WITNESS

Bayview

AMERICAN REVOLUTION

Signaling horn

Tea chest

Snuff box

Poster by Paul Revere

Regimental coat

"Brown Bess" musket

Drum

Continental money

American artillerymen loading a cannon

EYEWITNESS
AMERICAN REVOLUTION

Written by
STUART MURRAY

Telescope

Candle
lantern

 In association with the
Smithsonian Institution

DK | Penguin Random House

MEDIA PROJECTS INC.
Executive Editor C. Carter Smith
Managing Editor Carter Smith
Project Editor Aaron Murray
Designer Laura Smyth
Photo Researchers Robyn Bissette (S.I.), Athena Angelos

DK PUBLISHING
Editors Beth Sutinis, Elizabeth Hester, Carter Smith
Senior Art Editor Michelle Baxter
Creative Director Tina Vaughan
Jacket Art Director Dirk Kaufman
Publisher Andrew Berkhut
Production Manager Chris Avgherinos

RELAUNCH EDITION (DK UK)
Senior editor Chris Hawkes
Senior art editor Spencer Holbrook
US senior editor Margaret Parrish
Jacket editor Claire Gell
Jacket designer Laura Brim
Jacket design development manager Sophia MTT
Producer, pre-production Nikoleta Parasaki
Producer Vivienne Yong
Managing editor Linda Esposito
Managing art editor Philip Letsu
Publisher Andrew Macintyre
Publishing director Jonathan Metcalf
Associate publishing director Liz Wheeler
Design director Stuart Jackman

RELAUNCH EDITION (DK INDIA)
Senior editor Bharti Bedi
Project art editor Nishesh Batnagar
Editorial team Sheryl Sadana, Virien Chopra
DTP designer Pawan Kumar
Senior DTP designer Harish Aggarwal
Picture researcher Nishwan Rasool
Jacket designer Dhirendra Singh
Managing jackets editor Saloni Talwar
Pre-production manager Balwant Singh
Managing editor Kingshuk Ghoshal
Managing art editor Govind Mittal

First American Edition, 2002
This edition published in the United States in 2015 by DK Publishing
345 Hudson Street, New York, New York 10014

A Penguin Random House Company
16 17 18 19 10 9 8 7 6 5 4
004–280101–Sep/2015

Library of Congress Cataloging-in-Publication Data
Murray, Stuart, 1948-
American Revolution / by Stuart Murray.
American Revolution.—1st American ed.
p. cm. — (Dorling Kindersley eyewitness books)
Written in association with the Smithsonian Institution.
Summary: A visual guide, accompanied by text, to the people,
battles, and events of America's war for independence.

ISBN 978-1-4654-3858-4 (Paperback)
ISBN 978-1-4654-3859-1 (ALB)

1. United States—History—Revolution, 1775–1783—
Juvenile literature. [1. United States—History—Revolution, 1775-1783.] I. Dorling
Kindersley Publishing, Inc. II. Smithsonian Institution. III. Series.
E208 .A427 2002
973.3—dc21
2001047619

A WORLD OF IDEAS:
SEE ALL THERE IS TO KNOW
www.dk.com

Stoneware pitcher

Regimental flag

Pipe tomahawk

Colonial doll

Continental
infantryman

Liberty Cap
weathervane

Purple heart

Contents

George Washington's
sword and scabbard

British America

After the French war ended in 1763, peace and prosperity came to the Thirteen Colonies. By 1775, there were more than 2,700,000 colonists, and Philadelphia was a leading city in the British Empire. The ports of New York, Boston, and Charleston were booming. Each colony elected its own lawmaking assembly and had its own governor, although most were appointed by the king. Although proud British subjects, the colonials had been left to manage their own affairs for years. Now at peace with France and in possession of Canada, the British government intended to keep the American colonies under strict control.

The Thirteen Colonies

The Thirteen Colonies

Settlement growth in 1660

Settlement growth in 1700

Settlement growth in 1760

Atlantic Ocean

The American colonies that rose up against British rule lay along the Atlantic seaboard. European and African populations are shown for 1660 (dark green), 1700 (lighter green), and 1760 (lightest green).

New England

The four New England colonies of Rhode Island, Massachusetts, Connecticut, and New Hampshire relied on fishing, farming, shipbuilding, and seafaring. The unsettled region of Maine contained great trees to build ship masts. New England had many free laborers, as well as skilled artisans, such as carpenters and goldsmiths. There were few slaves.

Freedom suit

Young men often bound themselves to a tradesman for seven years as an apprentice to learn a skill. At the end, they might receive a "Freedom Suit," such as this one from Rhode Island.

A captain's diary

Captain Ashley Bowen of Marblehead, Massachusetts, recorded voyages and drew pictures of ships in his diary.

The colonial kitchen

A colonial family in Maiden, Massachusetts, gathered here for meals and prayers, or sat by the hearth to do handiwork or repair tools.

The Middle Colonies

New York, New Jersey, Pennsylvania, and Delaware had two large cities. Philadelphia was bustling with trade and commerce and was rich in colonial culture, such as music and art. New York was one of the busiest ports in the empire, and it was also a center of trade with native peoples.

A New Jersey eighteen pence banknote, issued in 1776

The State House
The colonial government of Pennsylvania met in Philadelphia at the State House, built 1732–1741.

Quaker farm
This prosperous 18th-century Pennsylvania farm shows a bustling summertime scene, with the family and hired hands plowing fields and managing horses and other livestock. In 1775, most colonials lived on farms.

The Southern Colonies

Most white people in Maryland, Virginia, North Carolina, South Carolina, and Georgia lived on family farms, but large-scale plantations dominated the economic and social systems. To produce cash crops—mainly tobacco, indigo, and rice—for market, the plantations relied on the forced labor of thousands of field slaves.

Rice scale

Rice hook and scale
Slaves cut husks with short-handled rice hooks. Next, the rice was pounded from the husks, then weighed in a scale.

Sickle

Virginia's capital
Virginia's capital, Williamsburg, boasted its own magnificent government building.

Slave quarters
Slave families on large Southern plantations sometimes lived in cabins, but were often crowded together in large barracks where there was little privacy.

War in the New World

Whenever France and England were at war, their American colonies also fought. The great Seven Years' War, which started in 1754, saw the two mighty empires clash on land and at sea. Known as the French and Indian War in America, the French won major battles early on. When, however, the British colonists and Redcoat soldiers outnumbered their foe they became too strong for the French, causing French strongholds, such as Quebec, to become British possessions. With the coming of peace, there would still be Indian uprisings, but the American colonies were strong as never before.

Grand strategist
Britain's prime minister William Pitt planned campaigns to capture French Canada.

Britain's American empire
Victory in the French and Indian War broke French power in America, bringing vast areas of eastern North America into the growing empire of English King George III.

Young Washington

George Washington, c.1772

Troops from Virginia were led by George Washington. While traveling through western Pennsylvania and the Ohio Valley, he wrote many reports for headquarters. At the age of 26, he was the only American-born officer to command a British brigade during the war.

Officer's writing set

Braddock's road
In July 1755, the arrogant British general Edward Braddock led an army of 1,400 soldiers against the French and Indians defending Fort Duquesne. His army was ambushed; however, a young George Washington organized the retreat of the survivors. But there were around 1,000 British-led casualties, including Braddock, who was buried under the road that was given his name.

Fall of Quebec

The last great French stronghold in Canada, Quebec City stood high above the Saint Lawrence River. In September 1759, General James Wolfe and his British troops rowed to an undefended cliff track, defeating the French, led by the Marquis de Montcalm. Both commanders died in battle.

Enduring mementos

Hundreds of British and French cannonballs littered the battlefields of this war. These were found at Fort Ticonderoga, a French-built bastion on Lake Champlain.

"King's Arrow," also called "Broad Arrow," means that the cannonball is royal property

French cannonball with royal fleur-de-lis symbol

Pontiac's Rebellion

After this war, some native peoples who had fought with the defeated French refused to accept British rule. Led by Ottawa chief Pontiac, several nations attacked British garrisons in May 1763 and laid siege to Fort Detroit. Warriors also drove out thousands of settlers. After hard fighting, British and colonial troops forced the nations to make peace in 1766.

Regimental coat

Major John Dagworthy, an officer in the 44th Regiment of Foot, wore this coat. He fought during the French and Indian War.

Pipe tomahawk, used both for smoking and war-making

Return of prisoners

In Pontiac's Rebellion, warriors rose up against the British and took prisoners. But upon defeat, chiefs of the Shawnee and Delaware nations met with British commander Colonel Henry Bouquet to arrange for the return of settlers.

Taxation without representation

In the 1760s, the British Parliament created acts that forced the colonies to pay tax on imports, such as sugar and tea. Since colonies did not elect representatives to Parliament, many Americans proclaimed that "taxation without representation" was illegal. Angry colonists refused to import British goods until the acts were lifted. In 1768, 4,000 Redcoats occupied Boston to punish the city for its resistance. Then in 1770, they fired on a rowdy mob— this is called the "Boston Massacre." Three years later, anti-Parliament leader Samuel Adams organized men to board a ship and dump its tea cargo into Boston Harbor.

"No Stamp Act"

A Virginian family's teapot makes clear their opposition to the 1765 Stamp Act requiring legal documents to have revenue stamps. Such stamps were kept in this leather box.

1766 Williamsburg teapot

"GR" stands for "George Rex" or "King George"

Tax collector's box

Revenue stamps

Boston Tea Party

Several ships carrying imported tea were attacked by colonial protesters. The most celebrated "tea party" was on December 16, 1773, when locals disguised as Indians threw 342 tea chests into Boston Harbor.

Tarred and feathered
Radical Bostonians attack a tax collector, coating him with hot tar and covering him with feathers.

The Boston Massacre

In 1770, soldiers were harassed by a threatening mob. Some angry Redcoats fired, killing five people. Put on trial, the soldiers were defended by attorney John Adams, who won acquittals for most, and only light punishment for others.

Samuel Adams
One of the most outspoken opponents of Parliament's taxation policies, Samuel Adams was also among the first people to consider independence from Britain.

Coffins for victims
This period engraving laments the Boston Massacre. Inscribed with the initials of the dead, "CJA" is for Crispus Attucks, the first African American killed in the Revolution.

Tea chest
This is a miniature replica of one of the East Indian tea boxes said to have been thrown into Boston Harbor.

Fiery propaganda
A poster by engraver Paul Revere depicts troops at the Boston Massacre firing together on command, which was not the case.

Opposing leaders

With King George III's support, Prime Minister Lord North led the government's military efforts to bring the colonies under control. Some British statesmen and generals, however, believed armed conflict would be a disaster for the empire. George Washington from Virginia was chosen to be commander in chief of the armies of Congress. New England Patriots John Adams, a political theorist, and John Hancock, a wealthy merchant, were among the first delegates to the Continental Congress. Along with Adams, legal expert John Jay from New York later traveled to France to represent America in international affairs.

Emblem of royalty
The British royal coat of arms includes the symbols of England, Scotland, Wales, and Ireland.

Lord Frederick North
Prime Minister North supported the tax on the colonies. He allied himself with King George and opposed men like the statesman Edmund Burke, who objected to Britain's colonial policies.

Sir William Howe
Spending most of his career in America, General Howe did not agree with British colonial policies. Yet from 1775, he led the British army in North America.

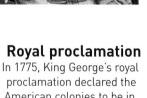

Royal proclamation
In 1775, King George's royal proclamation declared the American colonies to be in rebellion. Many colonists, he said, had forgotten the allegiance "they owe to the power that has protected and supported them."

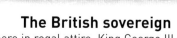

The British sovereign
Shown here in regal attire, King George III was just 22 when he took the throne in 1760. Americans petitioned the king to support the colonies' position, but he refused.

The American commander in chief

The Second Continental Congress appointed George Washington commander of all its forces because of his military experience. Washington believed the military must never take the reins of power in a republic. He also refused to become directly involved in politics while he was a soldier.

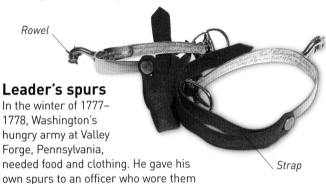

Rowel

Strap

Leader's spurs
In the winter of 1777–1778, Washington's hungry army at Valley Forge, Pennsylvania, needed food and clothing. He gave his own spurs to an officer who wore them on a ride of more than 300 miles to Boston to arrange for supplies.

At home in Virginia
Washington was a masterful horseman with a powerful physique. This, together with his wisdom and courage, helped him endure eight years as commander in chief. He is pictured at his beloved Mount Vernon plantation in Virginia. He left home at the start of the Revolution and did not return for six years.

The first signer
Evading British capture for not paying port fees, Boston Patriot John Hancock later became the president of the First and Second Continental Congresses. He was the first person to sign the Declaration of Independence.

A political mastermind
Lawyer John Adams of Massachusetts was an early challenger to British colonial policy. After helping draft the Declaration of Independence, Adams served in France as representative for the United States.

A Briton for America
Edmund Burke called, unsuccessfully, for the British Parliament to negotiate peacefully with the American colonies, rather than make war. He also championed the rights of other British colonies, including India.

John Jay
A brilliant New York attorney and jurist, Jay was a delegate to the Continental Congress and, later, an important diplomat. He was president of Congress from 1778–1779.

Pennsylvania coat of arms
The newly independent states had to create their own coats of arms. Pennsylvania chose to incorporate a ship, a plow, an eagle, and two white horses.

Revolution in the air

After the Boston Tea Party, Parliament voted in 1774 to place harsh regulations—called "Intolerable Acts" or "Coercive Acts"—on the colony. Set up in Philadelphia, the First Continental Congress united the colonies to stop buying British goods until Parliament repealed their laws. Americans made goods at home to replace British imports, and a Second Continental Congress was planned for 1775 if Britain did not change its policies. Meanwhile, Benjamin Franklin was returning to Philadelphia from London. He then believed the colonies must resist by force of arms.

Patrick Henry
A radical Virginia legislator, Henry believed King George had no right to rule America. He declared, "Give me liberty or give me death."

The Raleigh Tavern

In 1774, Virginia legislators met at Raleigh Tavern, named after the English adventurer Sir Walter Raleigh—misspelled "Ralegh" on its signboard. They agreed to boycott British goods, arm the colony, and send delegates to the First Continental Congress in Philadelphia.

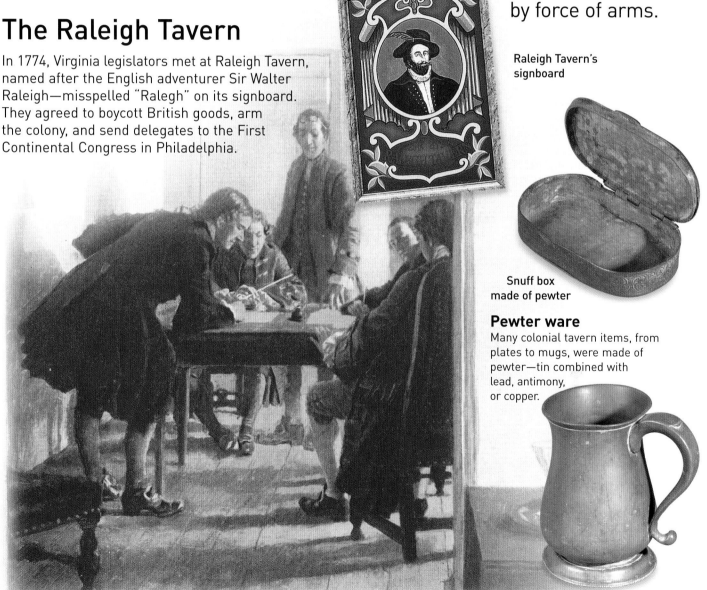

Raleigh Tavern's signboard

Snuff box made of pewter

Pewter ware
Many colonial tavern items, from plates to mugs, were made of pewter—tin combined with lead, antimony, or copper.

Drinking mug, or "tankard"

Preparing for conflict

The colonies armed to resist British oppression, and gunsmiths turned out muskets as fast as they could. These were called "flintlocks," because pulling the trigger caused a flint to strike a spark and fire the bullet. By early 1775, many Americans were ready to fight if the British kept suppressing colonial freedom.

Musket flints

Paper cartridge holds a bullet and gunpowder

Manufacturing muskets

American gunsmiths were skilled at making long-barreled hunting rifles, but soldiers needed short muskets that could take a bayonet. Rapid firing and bayonet charges by massed troops were essential to the success of an 18th-century army.

Spinning and weaving for liberty

Defying Parliament, Patriot women mobilized to spin thread and weave cloth to replace fabric normally imported from the British Empire. During the resistance period, these "Daughters of Liberty" worked to make the colonies more self-sufficient.

Multitalented statesman

Benjamin Franklin was a Philadelphia author and publisher, known for his experiments with electricity. Early on, he worked as a printer in England. He later returned to London as a colonial representative. In 1775, after an unsuccessful negotiation between Parliament and the colonists, he came back to America, expecting an armed struggle.

Portrait of Franklin

"Join or die"

Franklin's sketch shows the individual American colonies as a snake cut into pieces. For the snake—and the colonies—to survive, the parts must unite to work together.

Franklin ran this press in a London printshop

The Revolution begins

On April 18 1775, General Thomas Gage ordered Redcoats to look for stockpiles of colonial military supplies in Concord. Patriot leader Dr. Joseph Warren sent out riders to alert the militia. The next day—and after much shooting—the militia forced the marching Redcoats to retreat. The Americans laid siege to Boston, and the Revolution began.

"One if by land, two if by sea"
This is one of two candle lanterns placed in Boston's Old North Church's spire on the night of April 18, 1775. Two lanterns meant that Redcoats were crossing to the mainland by boat, not land.

Statue cast in bronze

The ride of Paul Revere
Revere alerted leaders John Hancock and Samuel Adams in Lexington of British plans. They escaped before the Redcoats came to arrest them.

Militia canteen
Inscribed with his initials, this wooden canteen belonged to Connecticut militia lieutenant Joseph Babcock. He responded to the "Lexington Alarm" on April 1775.

Shoulder strap for carrying canteen

The Minuteman
This statue honors the Massachusetts militiamen of 1775, who left their plows to fight against Redcoats marching out of Boston.

Lexington Green
British major John Pitcairn shouted "Disperse, ye rebels!" at defiant Minutemen gathered on Lexington Green, and a moment later firing broke out.

A bloody retreat

After reaching Concord, the Redcoats found themselves surrounded by thousands of armed militia. The march back to Boston 20 miles (32 km) away became a fierce, running battle all through the day.

Engraved silver decoration

Pitcairn's pistols

Under heavy rebel fire during the Redcoat retreat to Boston, Major Pitcairn's horse bolted, carrying away his pistols. They were captured by the militia.

Capture of Fort Ticonderoga

The once-mighty "Fort Ti" was in poor repair in 1775 and was occupied by only a few British soldiers, but it controlled strategic Lake Champlain. On May 10, Ethan Allen and Benedict Arnold with their rebel group attacked the fort. The British commander, Captain William Delaplace, was ordered to surrender or die—he surrendered.

Allen's compass

Ethan Allen used his sundial compass to reach "Fort Ti." This broadside announced the fort's capture in New York and New England.

British commander, Captain William Delaplace

Ethan Allen demands the surrender of Fort Ticonderoga.

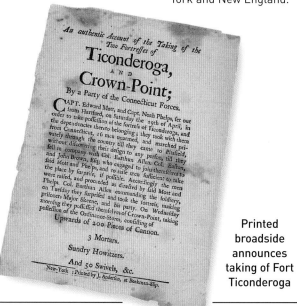

An authentic Account of the Taking of the Two Fortresses of

Ticonderoga,
AND
Crown-Point;

By a Party of the Connecticut Forces.

CAPT. Edward Mott, and Capt. Noah Phelps, set out from Hartford, on Saturday the 29th of April, in order to take possession of the fortress of Ticonderoga, and the dependencies thereto belonging; they took with them from Connecticut, 16 men unarmed, and marched privately through the country till they came to Pittsfield, without discovering their design to any person, till they fell in company with Col. Earthun Allen, Col. Easton, and John Brown, Esq; who engaged to join themselves to said Mott and Phelps, and to raise men sufficient to take the place by surprize, if possible. Accordingly the men were raised, and proceeded as directed by said Mott and Phelps. Col. Earthun Allen commanding the soldiery, on Tuesday they surprised and took the fortress, making prisoners Major Skeene, and his party. On Wednesday morning they possessed themselves of Crown-Point, taking possession of the Ordinance-Stores, consisting of

Upwards of 200 Pieces of Cannon.

3 Mortars.

Sundry Howitzers.

And 50 Swivels, &c.

New-York : Printed by J. Anderson, at Beekman-Slip.

Printed broadside announces taking of Fort Ticonderoga

Breed's Hill and Boston

Charles Town burns
British artillery in Boston and on warships fired red-hot cannonballs into Charles Town, setting it ablaze.

On June 16, 1775, hundreds of American militiamen dug fortifications on Breed's Hill, on the Charles Town peninsula, across the Charles River from Boston. The orders were to take nearby Bunker Hill, but rebel general Israel Putnam mistakenly seized Breed's Hill. General Gage's Redcoat regiments rowed across to attack but were pushed back twice before driving out the rebels. Two weeks later, General George Washington arrived to take command of the siege. In October, Gage was replaced with General William Howe. Late that winter, American artillery officer Henry Knox brought captured cannon to Washington, who aimed them at Boston. Howe had no choice but to evacuate the city.

Prescott calms his men
The British fired cannonballs into the entrenchments on Breed's Hill. When a man was killed, Colonel William Prescott leaped into the open, defying the fire.

Thomas Gage
General Gage was commander of British troops in the colonies. He had tried to avoid bloodshed, but after Lexington and Concord his army was trapped in Boston by thousands of angry rebels.

Attack on Breed's Hill
The Redcoats were twice driven back by the American defenders, who were finally overrun by a third British assault. Among the American dead was Dr. Joseph Warren; among the British was Major Pitcairn of the Royal Marines.

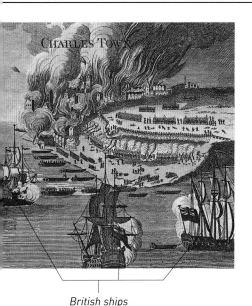

British ships

Washington reviews his troops
General George Washington took command of the rebel army, besieging Boston and soon building strong defenses to prevent the British from attacking.

Silver lion head pommel

Ivory grip

Putnam's sword
Patriot general Israel Putnam, a leader at the siege of Boston, owned this sword. It could have served as a weapon for combat or as a dress sword for formal occasions.

Steel blade, 27 in (68 cm) long

Rebel guns come to Boston
In the winter of 1775–1776, Henry Knox and his men carted 59 heavy guns to Boston. The artillery came from captured Fort Ticonderoga on Lake Champlain. It included mortars like this one, which could fire explosive shells high into the air and drop them onto a target.

Opening 8 in (20 cm) wide

Bronze mortar barrel weighs 700 lb (318 kg)

221 ft (67 m) tall

Powder horn
Soldiers kept gunpowder in hollowed-out horns that they often decorated with carved pictures. This horn was carried by Connecticut soldier Frederick Robbins during the siege of Boston.

"In Defence of Liberty" is carved into horn

Statue of rebel officer Colonel William Prescott

The British evacuate Boston
Before leaving, Howe's men destroyed what military supplies they could not take and threw some heavy cannon into the bay to prevent the Americans from getting them.

The "Bunker Hill" monument
In 1825, the people of Boston erected a monument to the battle at Breed's Hill.

Recruiting and training

In 1775, many Americans were members of militia companies—mainly social clubs that met a couple of times a year on "training days." When the Revolution started, men turned out with local militia for a short term of service. The states and Congress soon formed regiments that enlisted men for longer terms, teaching them military basics so they could maneuver on the battlefield. Their officers usually learned from drill manuals created for the rebel army. In time, American soldiers were able to stand up against the Redcoats and earned their respect.

The drummer
A company's drummer rapped out beats to prompt men to get up, to eat, and more. In battle, drum beats helped officers to move their troops.

Musician's pride
An American carried this drum throughout the Revolution. Drums had to be cared for so they could send loud signals to the troops.

First recruits for the Revolution
Officers taught unskilled volunteers how to handle muskets. By 1779, the best American regiments had uniforms and knew how to march. In later battles, these troops impressed both their French allies and British enemies.

Equipping the recruits

Militia carried their own firearms, while the regiments of the states and Congress used government-issue weapons. Congress and the states could not pay their troops, who usually suffered from few supplies. Most soldiers had to make their own bullets, using a mold that formed lead into balls.

Leather cartridge box for carrying ammunition

Bullet mold

A New Jersey soldier's wallet with state money

Handling a musket

As the American army developed, manuals were created to teach soldiers. This manual showed the steps for using a musket. In battle, soldiers stood in ranks, firing and reloading together on command.

Bullet

Red facings

Henry Knox

Before the Revolution, Henry Knox from Boston served in a militia artillery unit, learning from European books. He then trained other officers, who created artillerymen.

Buckskin breeches

Dragoons rode on horses to battle but usually dismounted to fight on foot. They wore buckskin breeches, which protected them from sharp branches and saddle sores.

Woolen jacket, colored blue with indigo dyes

A major's coat

Colonel Peter Gansevoort wore this uniform coat as commander of the 3rd New York Continental Regiment, made up of Dutch-descended soldiers from the Albany region.

Tough buckskin material

The two armies

Nicknamed "Redcoats" because of their red jackets, the British Army came from England, Scotland, Ireland, and Wales. They were joined by thousands of German soldiers called "Hessians," as well as American Loyalists. The American revolutionary army consisted of blue- or brown-coated regiments raised by the Continental Congress ("Continentals") and regiments belonging to the states. Civilians also often fought for the Revolution, as it swept into their region. Continental and British infantry carried smoothbore muskets and used the same basic battle tactics: massed firing by ranks and charging with the bayonet.

Informative badge
This badge indicated a British soldier of the 26th Regiment of Foot.

British grenadier
Each regiment had men trained to throw grenades. By 1775, these men were the elite troops, distinguished by their tall hats.

The Loyalists

A third of Americans remained loyal to Britain, and thousands fought for them. British officer Banastre Tarleton created a Loyalist cavalry legion, and Scottish colonists opposed to the Revolution created the 84th Royal Highland Emigrant Regiment.

84th Royal Highland Emigrant Regiment camp flag

Tarleton's Legion cavalryman

Triumphant occupation
Redcoats and their German allies parade through New York City while mounted officers and civilians look on. The city was captured by the king's forces in the summer of 1776. It was garrisoned by Redcoats, German troops, and Loyalists throughout the rest of the war.

Philadelphia Light Horse flag
The Philadelphia Light Horse was a distinguished Revolutionary unit made up of men from leading Pennsylvania families.

Revolutionary hat
American colonists usually wore three-corner hats called tricorns.

"Brown Bess" musket

Standing strong
The Continental infantryman, or "line soldier," was trained to stand firmly in rank during the heat of battle.

Drumbeat of discipline
The American army learned to march, form up in ranks, and behave like disciplined soldiers. The drum and fife set the rhythm for marching troops and sounded out battle commands and signals.

Artillery

American artillerymen were essential to Revolutionary forces. Forges from New England to Virginia made cannon and shot, but American gunners were always short of equipment. They often used guns and gear supplied by their French allies and reused British cannon balls picked up during battles.

Artillery gauge shows the angle at which the cannon barrel must be placed to hit a given target

Shell for explosive

"King's Arrow," states that cannonball is royal property

Rebel gun crew
These artillerymen swab their gun's hot muzzle with a damp sponge to stop sparks before reloading.

Early northern battles

Late in 1775, Americans marched against the Canadian towns of Montreal and Quebec to prevent the British Navy from landing a powerful force there. Led by New York generals Philip Schuyler and Richard Montgomery, the expedition captured Montreal in November and moved against Quebec. Then another expedition—commanded by Benedict Arnold of Connecticut—crossed the Maine wilderness in a brutal march to join them. But the combined American force was defeated at Quebec, and Montgomery was killed.

The taking of Ethan Allen
During the American campaign to capture Montreal in late 1775, British and Canadians trapped Ethan Allen and his volunteers.

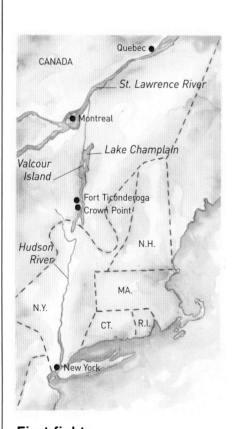

Montgomery's officer's sash

Earliest trophy
The flag of the British Seventh Regiment of Foot was the first ever captured by an American force. It was won in 1775.

First fights
Early clashes were in the Lake Champlain-Hudson River corridor—the main travel route between Canada and New York.

Montgomery falls
On December 31, 1775, American brigadier general Richard Montgomery was struck by cannon fire in the failed assault on Quebec. The second-in-command, Colonel Benedict Arnold, shown arriving at right, was also wounded in the defeat.

The little American fleet took shelter behind Valcour Island, firing bravely at the chain of British gunboats that were supported by warships in the foreground.

Battle of Valcour Island

In October 1776, Arnold forced the British fleet on Lake Champlain to attack his vessels at Valcour Island. Arnold's flotilla was destroyed, but its fierce resistance made the British fear the lake could not be captured before winter set in.

Out of a watery grave

The rebel gunboat *Philadelphia*, sunk at Valcour Island, was raised in 1935. It is the oldest American fighting vessel in existence.

Gunboat is 54 ft (16 m) long

12-pounder gun in its original carriage

Retreat to fight again

Several American vessels escaped from the Valcour Island defeat, but most were badly damaged. Some were even set on fire, so their crews had to run them aground and flee on foot.

Independence

In June 1776, the colonies were ready for independence. The Second Continental Congress, which met in Philadelphia, established a five-member drafting committee to write a document stating the reasons for separating from England. Thomas Jefferson composed the first draft for the committee to work on. When the document was presented to Congress, it contained a list of complaints against Great Britain, including the levying of taxes without American consent. The 56 delegates debated the wording until July 4, finally producing the Declaration of Independence. The formal copy was ready for signing in August.

Thomas Jefferson
The 33-year-old Jefferson drafted a document that would convince the colonists to unite as one nation.

Drawer for papers, pens, and inkwell

Jefferson's desk
Jefferson used this folding portable writing desk to draft the Declaration. After many hours of solitary thinking, he returned to his desk to compose. The drawer holds writing implements, such as quills and ink.

The labor of liberty
Discarded pages litter the floor, as Benjamin Franklin (left) and John Adams (center) helped Jefferson (right) prepare the document.

Common sense
In 1776, the 50-page pamphlet *Common Sense* by philosopher Thomas Paine stirred up an American belief in liberty. He asserted that government was created to serve the people and foster their happiness, not oppress them. He said, "the last cord is now broken" between America and Britain.

COMMON SENSE;

ADDRESSED TO THE

INHABITANTS

OF

AMERICA,

On the following interesting

SUBJECTS.

I. Of the Origin and Design of Government in general, with concise Remarks on the English Constitution.

II. Of Monarchy and Hereditary Succession.

III. Thoughts on the present State of American Affairs.

IV. Of the present Ability of America, with some miscellaneous Reflections.

Man knows no Master save creating HEAVEN,
Or those whom choice and common good ordain.
THOMSON.

PHILADELPHIA;
Printed, and Sold, by R. BELL, in Third-Street.
MDCCLXXVI.

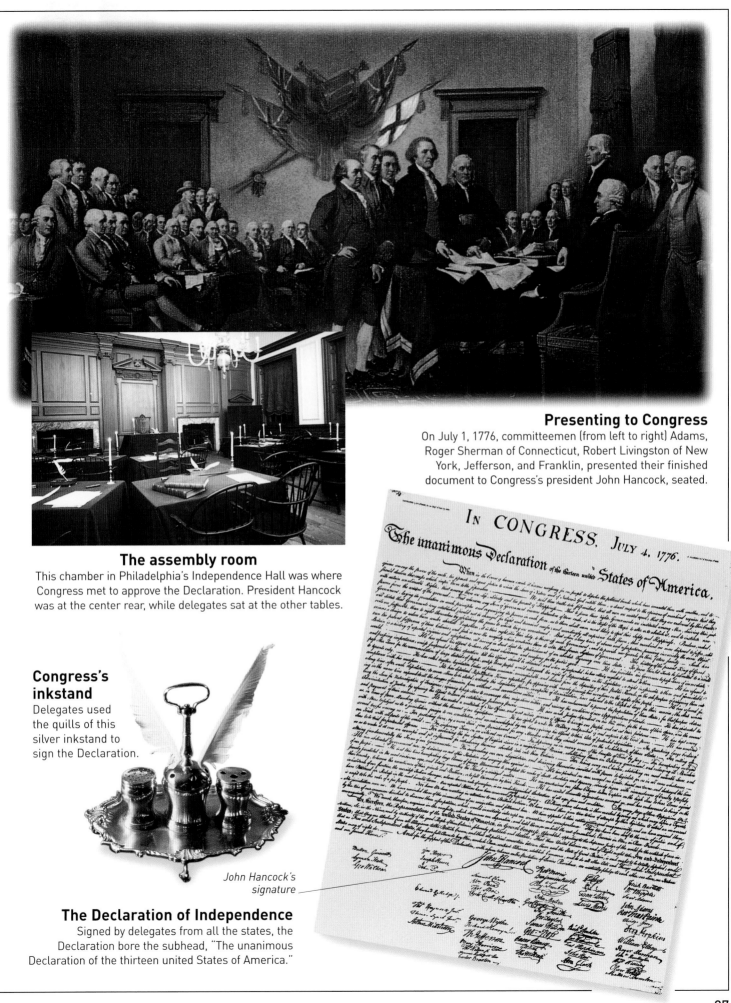

Presenting to Congress
On July 1, 1776, committeemen (from left to right) Adams, Roger Sherman of Connecticut, Robert Livingston of New York, Jefferson, and Franklin, presented their finished document to Congress's president John Hancock, seated.

The assembly room
This chamber in Philadelphia's Independence Hall was where Congress met to approve the Declaration. President Hancock was at the center rear, while delegates sat at the other tables.

Congress's inkstand
Delegates used the quills of this silver inkstand to sign the Declaration.

John Hancock's signature

The Declaration of Independence
Signed by delegates from all the states, the Declaration bore the subhead, "The unanimous Declaration of the thirteen united States of America."

On the battlefield

Signal horn
Drums, whistles, fifes, bagpipes, and horns were used to send orders to troops. A signaling horn could be heard a long way over the din of battle.

After evacuating Boston in the spring of 1776, the British under Howe sent a small expedition to Charleston, South Carolina, but it was driven back. Next, he invaded New York to defeat Washington's army, who retreated ultimately to Pennsylvania, and it seemed Philadelphia would also soon fall to the British. But on Christmas Eve, Washington counterattacked, defeating German troops at Trenton, and a few days later he triumphed over a British force at Princeton. The Patriot army marched to the New Jersey hills, where it would remain for the winter. Washington was striking back.

Bullet mold
Soldiers made ammunition using molds, such as this one carved from soapstone. After pouring molten lead into the channels, the lead was then cooled to produce musket balls.

A failed British attack

In June 1776, British commander Sir Henry Clinton led nine warships and 2,500 Redcoats against Charleston. His troops tried to attack the fort on Sullivan's Island, which guarded the harbor, but they were forced back. The fort's guns pounded the warships and the invasion was called off and Charleston was saved.

Great defender
On Sullivan's Island, South Carolina's Colonel William Moultrie had only 21 guns against 10 enemy warships. But his men fired more accurately than the British.

The Battle of Long Island

In August 1776, Sir William Howe sent 20,000 soldiers against Washington's 8,000-man army, which was fortified on Long Island. The Patriots were defeated and trapped against the East River, but at night Washington evacuated his army to Manhattan Island.

Steel blade, 5¾ in (14.6 cm) long

A soldier's razor

When not on the march, Revolutionary soldiers of both armies used straight razors to keep their faces clean-shaven.

Grenadier cap

Like the British, some Patriot troops wore tall caps to show they were in an elite company called grenadiers. This cap belonged to a soldier of the 26th Continental Infantry Regiment, which fought at Trenton in 1776.

Grenade design

Rising from defeat

Driven from New York in 1776, Washington's army retreated across the Delaware River. On Christmas Day, he crossed back over the ice-choked river and surprised German soldiers at Trenton. The victory stunned the British high command, who realized the war was not yet over.

A second stunning blow

In January 1777, the British general Lord Cornwallis came after Washington to avenge the Trenton defeat. But Washington's 5,200-man army beat Cornwallis's soldiers at Princeton.

Map labels

Quebec

Montreal

Maine (part of Mass.)

CANADA

St. Lawrence River

Lake Champlain

Ft. Ticonderoga

Lake Ontario

N.H.

Saratoga

Lexington & Concord

Boston

Oriskany

Albany

Ma.

New York

Hudson River

R.I.

Ct.

Newport

Lake Erie

Ft. Detroit

Newburgh
West Point
Stony Point

Delaware R

Pennsylvania

N.J.

Long Island

Ft. Lee

Battle of Long Island

Morristown

New York City (Ft. Washington)

Princeton

Monmouth

Germantown

Trenton

Valley Forge

Philadelphia

Brandywine

Md.

Chesapeake Bay

De.

Virginia

Williamsburg

Yorktown

Allegheny Mountains

Guilford Courthouse

North Carolina

Cowpens

South Carolina

Charleston

Georgia

Savannah

Atlantic Ocean

N
W E
S

KEY
- Battle site
- Town or fort

EAST FLORIDA (SPAIN)

The greatest battles

In August 1777, Sir William Howe and 15,000 British troops defeated Washington's army of 10,500 at Brandywine Creek, yet the rebel army remained intact. In September, Washington attacked British encampments at Germantown, Pennsylvania, which drove the enemy back, but American inexperience allowed the British to win the day. There was still hope for the Revolutionary cause, however, as Burgoyne was captured at Saratoga in October. During the following winter of 1777–1778, Washington's men practiced battle maneuvers at Valley Forge. By summer, they were ready to attack the new enemy commander, Sir Henry Clinton. The British General abandoned Philadelphia, sending his army toward New York. Then, Washington attacked him at Monmouth, and the battle ended a draw. Washington next moved his army to the Hudson Valley to continue the siege of New York City.

Halberd

Iron spontoons

Wooden shaft

Lethal arms
Spontoons showed rank and were used in close combat. At first, sergeants had halberds and officers carried spontoons. In time, halberds were replaced by swords or muskets with bayonets.

The course of war
In 1777, Howe defeated Washington at Brandywine and Germantown. But Howe was forced to resign for failing to destroy Washington's army and not supporting Burgoyne, who was captured at Saratoga. The new British commander, Sir Henry Clinton, left Philadelphia in mid-1778 and returned to New York. He shifted the action to the South in the hope of pacifying that region.

Attacking the Chew House at Germantown

American assaults at Germantown drove back the enemy, but 120 Redcoats made a stand in the Chew's family house. Heavy fog caused some Americans to fire on each other, resulting in panic, and Washington's army retreated.

Anthony Wayne

Pennsylvanian Wayne was known as "Mad Anthony" because of his reckless spirit. Fighting in several campaigns, he won fame in 1779 for storming Stony Point on the Hudson.

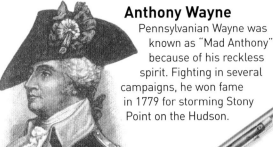

Daniel Morgan

A skilled commander and rifleman, General Morgan served against Burgoyne and Howe in the battles of 1777–1778. His great victory was against a 1,100-strong force in 1781 at Cowpens, South Carolina.

Touch hole

"Brown Bess" musket

Brush

Pick

Touch hole pick and brush

Red musket

Nicknamed "Brown Bess," this musket fired a .75-caliber lead ball, accurate to about 75 yards. The soldier carried a pick and brush to clean residue that clogged the touch hole, which had to be clear for the spark to ignite the charge.

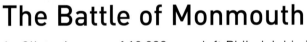

The Battle of Monmouth

As Clinton's army of 10,000 men left Philadelphia in June 1778, Washington attacked it. He sent General Charles Lee with 6,400 men but Lee lacked confidence and retreated against Clinton's brigades. Furious at Lee, Washington and 7,000 men arrived to stop the retreat. Each side lost about 360 men. The Redcoats held the battlefield but withdrew in the night, heading for New York City. Monmouth was the last major battle in the North.

Molly Pitcher fights at Monmouth

Women who carried water for their men in battle were called "Molly Pitchers." The most famous Molly was Mary Ludwig Hays, who took the place of her wounded husband at Monmouth. After the battle, Washington himself commended her bravery.

Washington stops Lee's retreat

As General Lee retreated with his division, Washington arrived and demanded to know why. Lee, a former British dragoon officer, claimed his men could not stand against such a formidable enemy. Washington exploded in anger, sent Lee to the rear, and hurried his troops into battle order. Lee was court-martialed and suspended from duty.

Victory at Saratoga

In June 1777, a royal army journeyed from Canada over Lake Champlain. General John Burgoyne led a force of 7,000, from Redcoats to Indian warriors. He aimed to capture Albany, New York, and meet the British army operating around New York City. In July, he captured Fort Ticonderoga. They advanced down the Hudson River, but in August part of the army was defeated near Bennington, Vermont. In October, Burgoyne's entire force was defeated in Saratoga, signaling the turning point in the Revolution.

A corridor of war
The Lake Champlain-Hudson River region was a strategic military zone. Burgoyne thought he could divide New England from the rest of the colonies by capturing it.

John Burgoyne
The dashing General Burgoyne won the confidence of King George III, who placed him in command of the royal Northern Army for the 1777 campaign. But the Americans surrounded and captured his expedition at Saratoga, New York.

American sharpshooter

General Simon Fraser is shot

The fall of General Fraser
The most experienced British officer at Saratoga was General Simon Fraser, who was killed by an American sharpshooter firing from high in a tree. Fraser had served in the colonies through the French and Indian War and was much loved by his men.

Sharpshooting rifle

The most accurate firearm of the day, rifles were used by rangers and sharpshooters in both armies. It was loaded with black powder poured into the barrel, followed by a lead ball pushed in with a starter and forced all the way down with a ramrod.

Ramrod

Wooden rifle ball starter

Powder measure

Victorious Gates

Although he received credit for the Saratoga victory, commander General Horatio Gates stayed at headquarters, while Arnold and others led his troops into action.

The heroic Arnold

Before Benedict Arnold betrayed the cause of the Revolution and joined the British, he was an excellent American general. While leading a successful attack against German defenders, he was shot and severely wounded in the leg.

A prize of war

Captured British guns were often sent to the artillery-weak American army. This cannon was inscribed with the proud words: "Surrendered by the Convention of Saratoga, October 17, 1777."

Redcoat kettle drum

Each British regiment had musicians that led the way in marches and parades; in battle, they set aside instruments to carry wounded men. This kettle drum of the Ninth Regiment of Foot was captured by the Americans at Saratoga.

Burgoyne offers his sword in defeat

Upon surrendering, Burgoyne offers his sword to General Gates. At right, American officers look on, with royal officers at left. Following military tradition, Gates only touched the sword, then allowed Burgoyne to keep it out of respect for a gallant opponent.

Frontier attacks

Many native peoples were loyal to Great Britain because they feared a Patriot triumph would lead to mass white migration into their lands. Early in the war, loyal Indians in the South were defeated by Patriots, but in New York's Mohawk Valley, Iroquois under Chief Joseph Brant joined loyal whites and Redcoats to raid Patriot strongholds. But Virginia frontiersmen, led by George Rogers Clark, invaded the northwest in 1778–1779, capturing the British governor and reducing attacks from that region.

Joseph Brant
Called Thayendanegea by his Iroquois people, Brant was a Loyalist during the Revolution. He became secretary to the British superintendent of Indian affairs and later commanded Iroquois forces fighting Patriots on the New York frontier.

Gifts of honor
Gorgets worn around the neck indicated rank. The silver gorget with a strap is believed to have belonged to Iroquois Joseph Brant.

Slaughter at Oriskany
In 1777, Patriot general Nicholas Herkimer and 800 militiamen tried to protect Fort Stanwix, which had come under attack from the British. En route, Loyalists and allied Indian tribes ambushed Herkimer's force near Oriskany, New York, culminating in a bloody battle.

The daring Long Knives

Patriot frontiersmen of Kentucky and western Virginia were nicknamed "Long Knives" because they carried large knives. In 1778, 200 Long Knives led by George Rogers Clark journeyed to the Old Northwest—Ohio, Illinois, and Indiana. Clark captured forts at Vincennes and Kaskaskia and imprisoned Redcoat commander Lieutenant Colonel Henry Hamilton. As a result, the British Army held only Fort Detroit in the Northwest.

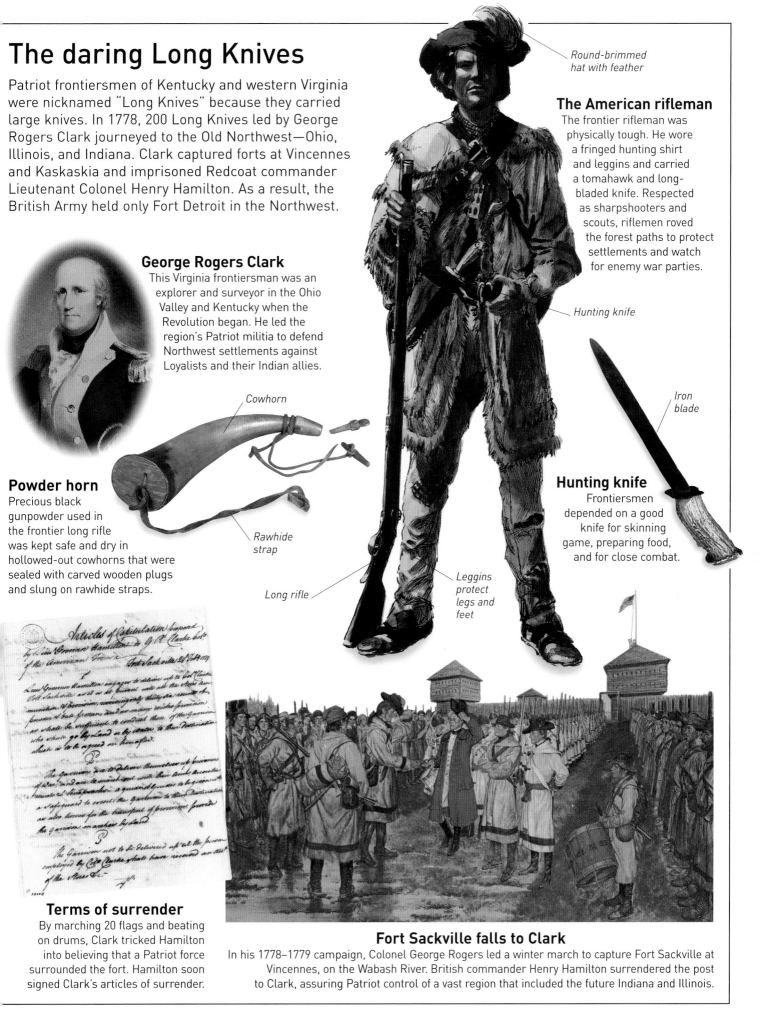

Round-brimmed hat with feather

The American rifleman
The frontier rifleman was physically tough. He wore a fringed hunting shirt and leggins and carried a tomahawk and long-bladed knife. Respected as sharpshooters and scouts, riflemen roved the forest paths to protect settlements and watch for enemy war parties.

Hunting knife

George Rogers Clark
This Virginia frontiersman was an explorer and surveyor in the Ohio Valley and Kentucky when the Revolution began. He led the region's Patriot militia to defend Northwest settlements against Loyalists and their Indian allies.

Cowhorn

Iron blade

Powder horn
Precious black gunpowder used in the frontier long rifle was kept safe and dry in hollowed-out cowhorns that were sealed with carved wooden plugs and slung on rawhide straps.

Rawhide strap

Hunting knife
Frontiersmen depended on a good knife for skinning game, preparing food, and for close combat.

Long rifle

Leggins protect legs and feet

Terms of surrender
By marching 20 flags and beating on drums, Clark tricked Hamilton into believing that a Patriot force surrounded the fort. Hamilton soon signed Clark's articles of surrender.

Fort Sackville falls to Clark
In his 1778–1779 campaign, Colonel George Rogers led a winter march to capture Fort Sackville at Vincennes, on the Wabash River. British commander Henry Hamilton surrendered the post to Clark, assuring Patriot control of a vast region that included the future Indiana and Illinois.

Winter soldier

Although both armies usually stayed in quarters during the worst winter weather, Washington was always on the alert for a surprise enemy attack. In the winter of 1778–1779, his little army was weak and hungry when it went into camp at Valley Forge, Pennsylvania. By spring, however, it emerged as a solid fighting force. Since the army usually had a different camp each year, the men also had to build log huts and shelters for livestock, equipment, and supplies.

Baron Friedrich Von Steuben
A Prussian nobleman, Von Steuben joined Washington's army at Valley Forge and drilled troops. In turn, the officers he trained taught their own men what they had learned.

Von Steuben's manual
Baron Von Steuben wrote a drill manual that was used to train the entire American army.

Freezing duty
As winter encampments had to be guarded at all times, sentries like this soldier, bundled themselves in blanket coats and wrapped their heads and feet in cloth rags.

Leather strap

Ice creepers
Bound with leather straps to shoes or boots, these iron cleats allowed a soldier to cross a frozen surface without slipping.

Visiting the troops
General Washington, left, rides out from headquarters to see how well his men are keeping warm and dry. Accompanied by French volunteer the Marquis de Lafayette, Washington makes sure the sentries are alert and on guard, like the soldier standing at attention before him.

Washington's life guard

On duty at a winter encampment, this soldier is a member of the corps that protected General Washington. Called the "Life Guard," this unit of specially chosen men numbered between 180–250 during the war.

Officer's uniform

The soldier's winter home

A log hut held 12 men, who slept on bunks three high. Loose straw covered with a blanket served as bedding. A soldier's few personal effects included clothing and a Bible.

Officer's trunk

The limited possessions an American officer brought with him could be carried in this leather-covered trunk. The exterior brass tacks protected it during rough handling.

Mouth harp

This instrument made a twanging sound when it was held between the teeth and the steel vibrator was plucked.

Iron mouth harp

Missing steel vibrator would be here

Building log huts in the snow

It was usually already cold and snow had fallen by the time the army withdrew from the field after a warm-weather campaign. Using oxen, troops had to haul heavy loads and flatten roadways to build huts for their winter encampments.

Symbols of freedom

The early flag of the United States had 13 stripes to represent the states and the Union Jack to honor the colonies' British heritage. When independence became the goal, Congress adopted a new flag with a field of stars for the states. Philadelphia's "Liberty Bell," which rang out to celebrate the Declaration of Independence, became a symbol of the Revolution. Another celebration of liberty was "Yankee Doodle," a tune sung by Redcoats that mocked Americans. Patriots composed new verses to express the pride of the revolutionaries.

The national colors

The first American flag was the "Grand Union" flag, combining the British Union Jack and 13 stripes for each state. On June 14, 1777, Congress resolved that the flag would be 13 stars on a blue field and 13 red and white stripes. They did not agree on a final arrangement of the stars, so various designs were used at first. One had stars in a circle, while others had the stars arranged as seen above.

The Betsy Ross tale

In 1777, the new United States needed a "national color" to replace the "Grand Union" flag that bore the Union Jack. Once Congress approved the design, legend has it that Philadelphia seamstress Elizabeth "Betsy" Ross was asked by General Washington to sew the first national flag.

Liberty bell

In 1751, Pennsylvania ordered a bell from England for the new state house. Inscribed "Proclaim Liberty thro' all the land," the bell cracked the first time it was rung and had to be repaired. In use for more than 75 years, in 1776 it rang joyously for the Declaration of Independence. It cracked again in 1835.

The famous crack

Song of defiance

Early in the Revolution, Redcoats sang "Yankee Doodle" to mock New England "Yankee"militiamen, calling them "doodles," or fools. When the Yankees triumphed in battle, they insulted the British by singing the "Yankee Doodle" melody with new, patriotic words.

Ropes for tension

Leather lugs for tightening ropes

Hoops

Drum body, painted

Militia fife

Fife and drum of freedom

This military fife was played by militiaman Jonathan Curtis of Concord, Massachusetts. The drum belonged to militiaman William Diamond of Lexington, Massachusetts, who beat out the signal for his companions on Lexington Common on April 19, 1775, where the war's first shots were fired.

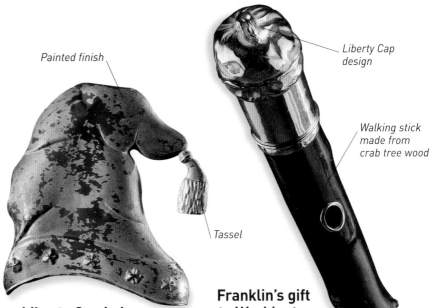

Painted finish

Liberty Cap design

Walking stick made from crab tree wood

Tassel

Liberty Cap in iron

The knitted "Liberty Cap" was one of the symbols of the American Revolution. Worn as a statement of a radical political position, it was so popular that iron weather vanes were forged into the cap's shape, painted, and fixed proudly to barns and houses.

Franklin's gift to Washington

Benjamin Franklin specified in his will that his "fine crab tree walking stick with a gold head curiously wrought in the form of a cap of liberty" would be left to his friend General Washington. Franklin died in 1790.

France becomes an ally

A noble volunteer
In 1777, the modest French nobleman Marquis de Lafayette volunteered to help Washington. He offered to do whatever was needed. An excellent officer, he quickly became a general.

Short on military supplies, cash, and a navy, America needed allies. Beaten by Britain in the Seven Years' War, France was eager to help America. By mid-1776, France was secretly sending financial aid and supplies to support the Revolution, but more was needed. That year, Benjamin Franklin traveled to Paris to arrange a formal alliance with King Louis XVI. The Americans befriended the foreign minister Comte de (Count of) Vergennes, who masterminded France's efforts. By early 1778, a state of war existed between France and Britain. Eventually, more than 12,000 French troops would fight in America under commander Comte de Rochambeau.

Golden Louis
This French Louis D'Or gold piece and thousands more just like it arrived in America as a gift from France. The valuable "Louis" helped turn the tide in favor of the Revolution.

Crown

Image of King Louis XVI

French royal symbol
The fleur-de-lis, or "lily flower," decorated the coat of arms of the Bourbons, the French royal house.

Fleur-de-lis

Franklin at the French court
Scientist, philosopher, and diplomat, Benjamin Franklin was famous throughout France and warmly welcomed when he and the American delegation arrived in 1777. They were presented at the royal palace of Versailles to King Louis XVI, who approved aid to help the Revolution.

John Adams inspects French marines

The French army included several regiments of Irish-born troops, who often wore red uniforms. In this painting, American diplomat John Adams is inspecting Irishmen on the coast of France. They have volunteered as marines for the American warship *Bonhomme Richard*.

Lock from a French musket

This iron gunlock, the firing mechanism of a French musket, was found on a Revolutionary War battlefield. The cock holds a piece of flint that strikes the steel frizzen when the trigger is pulled, making a spark that ignites gunpowder in the pan and fires the bullet in the barrel of the musket.

Gap for flint

Pan

Cock

Frizzen

French sword

There were many types and sizes of sword, from the cavalryman's heavy saber to this light and slender French "small sword," ideal for an infantry officer.

The French commander

The leader of French troops in North America, Jean Baptiste Donatien de Vimeur, Comte de Rochambeau, commanded more than 7,000 well-equipped French soldiers. He treated Washington and the Americans as equals: at one point, Rochambeau opened his army's war chest to Washington, offering to share half of the money it held.

Comte de Vergennes

French foreign minister Charles Gravier, Comte de Vergennes, helped with secret contributions of funds and supplies to the American revolutionaries. France's support of America led to all-out war in 1778.

The war at sea

Americans lacked warships but soon tried a new invention: the submarine. In 1776, the *Turtle* attempted to attach a bomb beneath a warship in New York Harbor, but when the plan failed, submarines were forgotten for decades. British ships dominated American waters until the French fleet arrived to challenge them in 1778. While huge sea battles raged between French and British fleets in Caribbean and European waters, the Americans had triumphs of their own. Congress authorized private ship owners, called "privateers," to attack enemy vessels.

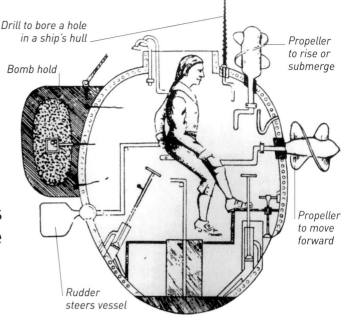

Drill to bore a hole in a ship's hull

Bomb hold

Propeller to rise or submerge

Propeller to move forward

Rudder steers vessel

Underwater attack
The first combat submarine, called the *Turtle*, went into action in September 1776 in New York Harbor. Its one-man crew tried unsuccessfully to attach a bomb to the hull of a British warship.

A French admiral
In 1778, Admiral Charles Comte d'Estaing failed to seal off New York Harbor. Next, he refused to aid an American attack on Rhode Island, and could not wipe out weaker enemy squadrons in the Caribbean. He was wounded in a defeat at Savannah in 1779.

Naval flags
The British Royal Navy's red flag has a Union Jack in the corner. Independent states designed flags for their own warships. South Carolina's ships carried flags with a rattlesnake and a stern warning.

Royal Navy ensign

DONT TREAD ON ME

South Carolina naval flag

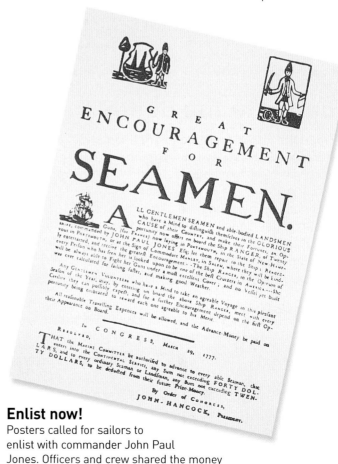

Enlist now!
Posters called for sailors to enlist with commander John Paul Jones. Officers and crew shared the money made from captured and sold enemy vessels.

The *Raleigh*

The 32-gun frigate *Raleigh* was one of the 13-ship fleet of the first Continental Navy. Frigates were fast, medium-sized warships carrying between 28 and 60 guns. *Raleigh* was captured by the British, who copied its design for their own vessels.

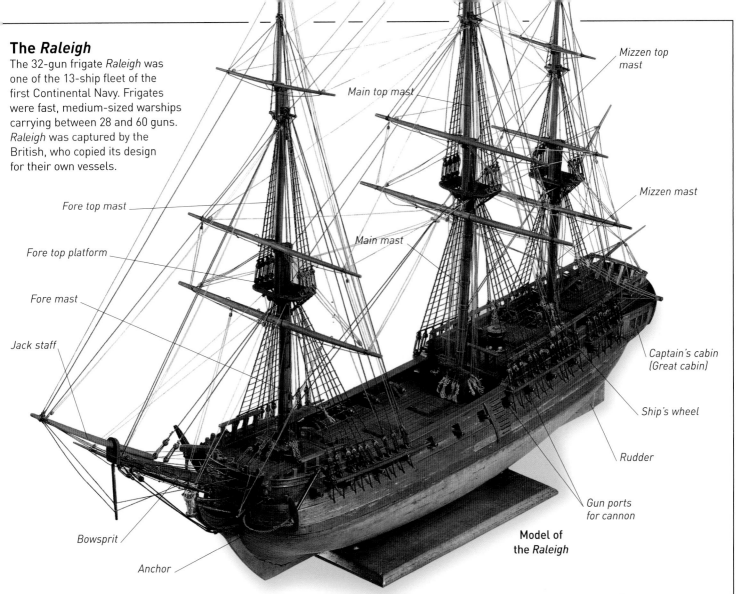

Mizzen top mast

Main top mast

Fore top mast

Mizzen mast

Fore top platform

Main mast

Fore mast

Captain's cabin (Great cabin)

Jack staff

Ship's wheel

Rudder

Gun ports for cannon

Bowsprit

Anchor

Model of the *Raleigh*

A battle to the death

In 1779, John Paul Jones led his *Bonhomme Richard* in a fatal battle with the enemy's flagship, *Serapis*—misspelled "*Seraphis*" in the artwork (right). As the British captain saw the American ship sinking, he demanded that Jones surrender. Jones answered, "I have not yet begun to fight!" He captured the *Serapis* as his own vessel went down. In 1787, Congress honored Jones with a medal for his service.

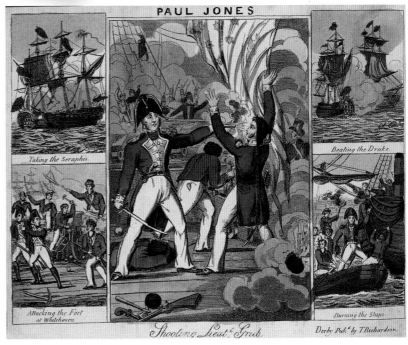

Scenes from the career of John Paul Jones
The central image shows Jones attacking one of his officers, who wanted to surrender during battle with the *Serapis*. Jones seized the enemy ship (top left).

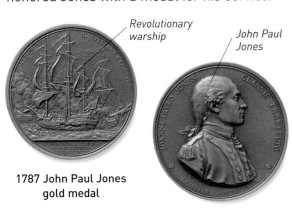

Revolutionary warship

John Paul Jones

1787 John Paul Jones gold medal

Embattled New York

In 1775, Patriot activists were outnumbered by Loyalists in New York City. After losing Boston early in 1776, Sir William Howe captured New York that summer, driving out Washington and the rebel sympathizers. Patriots burned down part of New York, but Redcoats held on to the city for the rest of the war. Thousands of Loyalists came, causing overcrowding and food shortages. After peace was made, on November 25, 1783, or "Evacuation Day," Washington and his few remaining officers rode in to take back the city.

Symbols of resistance
Before the Revolution, Patriots and Redcoats clashed in New York City. Liberty Poles were raised by Patriots and torn down by soldiers after bloody fights.

Light entertainment
New York was known for its lively theaters. The most popular musical play of the period was *The Beggar's Opera*. These comedies made fun of high society.

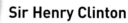

Alexander Hamilton
Born in the West Indies, Hamilton came to New York in his teens. An active Patriot, he later became Washington's military secretary and was known as the "Pen of the Army."

Sir Henry Clinton
Known for his bravery, Clinton was Howe's top lieutenant general during the invasion of New York in 1776. In 1778, he succeeded Howe in overall command, but resigned in 1781 after failing to achieve victory over the revolutionaries.

Downing the king's statue
In July 1776, the Declaration of Independence was read to the American army in New York and a mob tore down a statue of King George.

German troops help the British
In 1776, German soldiers captured New York, then occupied Manhattan.

The Great Fire

As the British moved into New York in 1776, Washington wanted to prevent use of the city as a British base. Although it is not known if direct orders were given, rebels soon set fire to much of New York.

Flint

Tinder lighter
This lighter sparked to ignite tinder, a flammable material kept dry in a box. Burning tinder ignited kindling to start a fire. A steel striker was struck against flint to create a spark.

Tinder box

Steel striker

Burning and killing
As buildings in New York burned on September 21, 1776, British soldiers beat and bayonetted suspected arsonists. For years to come, there were not enough houses for occupying soldier and civilians.

Flying the Stars and Stripes
British soldiers leaving New York nailed the Union Jack to a flagpole. While Redcoats watched, a Patriot climbed up, tore off the flag, and put up the Stars and Stripes instead.

Triumphant entry into the city
On November 25, 1783, or "Evacuation Day," Washington and some officers took possession of New York City from the departing British.

Spies and traitors

During the Revolution, secret messages were sometimes written in code and often hidden in shoe heels. Captured spies were hanged, such as the 20-year-old Continental officer Nathan Hale, who was caught in New York in 1776. Through much of the war, Washington counted on Major Benjamin Tallmadge to meet secretly with undercover agents and give them money. New Jersey-born Patience Wright, who lived in England during the war, hid messages inside her own sculptures and shipped them to American Patriots. General Benedict Arnold was the most notorious traitor to the Revolution. His plan to surrender West Point in 1780 was uncovered just in time.

Washington's spymaster
Dragoon major Benjamin Tallmadge was a link between Washington and secret agents in and around British-controlled New York City. In 1780, he exposed Benedict Arnold's plot to betray West Point, a key fort on the Hudson River.

A Patriot's cloak
During Washington's 1775–1776 siege of Boston, Deborah Champion wore this hooded cloak to carry messages and the army payroll secretly to rebel troops there.

Coins for conspiracies
There were very few coins in Revolutionary America, and what there were included Spanish silver reales, sometimes cut into several pieces. Spies had to be paid, and secret messengers needed cash to buy horses or pay for ferries or food, so any silver money would do.

His life for liberty
In mid-1776, Patriot officer Nathan Hale slipped into occupied New York City disguised as a schoolmaster. Caught then sentenced to be hanged, legend has it he said, "I regret that I have but one life to give for my country!"

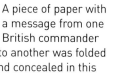

Hollow bullet
A piece of paper with a message from one British commander to another was folded and concealed in this hollow silver bullet.

Silver coin cut into a quarter

Spying artist
Famous for making heads out of putty or wax, American Patience Wright owned a studio in London. As a supporter of the rebel cause, she talked to her subjects about British military plans, then passed on to Patriot agents whatever she learned.

Captured and exposed

On September 21, 1780, General Benedict Arnold secretly handed documents outlining fortifications and troop information to British major John André. With the message hidden in the heel of his boot, André was on his way back to British lines when he was stopped by rebel sentries. He was hanged as a spy.

Turncoat hero

With such success on the battlefield, General Arnold despised Congress for placing other officers ahead of him in rank. In 1780, the disillusioned general conspired to help the British capture West Point. When the plot was discovered, he escaped to join the British forces. He eventually went to England with his wife and children.

Document box

Important papers, military dispatches, and correspondence needed to be sheltered from the elements and prying eyes. This leather, brass, and canvas strongbox could be locked securely to protect its contents.

A loyal wife

Philadelphian Peggy (Shippen) Arnold was with her husband during the West Point espionage affair, but she was not judged a coconspirator. Afterward, she and their son, Edward, were allowed to rejoin Arnold behind British lines.

Benedict Arnold

Once immensely popular, in 1780 Arnold became the most hated turncoat when he tried to arrange the British capture of West Point. He escaped and joined the royal forces, then left America for Britain in 1781.

The home front

During the Revolution, Americans were divided into three camps: Patriots, Loyalists, and neutrals. Only a few thousand people on each side made up the armies. Loyalists gathered in cities that were British strongholds, while Patriots gained control of most of the countryside. Neutrals were often harassed by both armies, and in land between the hostile forces no one was safe from raiders and pillagers. Yet, life went on and families worked hard to survive and make the best of things. Some even continued to meet their neighbors at their local public house.

Hoeing the land
To keep weeds down, farmers worked the soil with iron hoes attached to stout handles.

Farm work goes on
Most Americans lived on farms during the Revolution, and planting and harvesting continued according to the seasons. The crops depended on the simple plow, held by the strong-backed farmer while draft animals pulled.

Redcoat pillaging
Although soldiers were not encouraged to raid farmsteads and steal from houses, they often did. These Redcoats, above, are ransacking a house in New Jersey, while the distraught family looks on.

The public house

Taverns and inns were known as "public houses," where folk gathered to drink and eat, read newspapers, share stories, gossip, and gamble on dice and cards. They also offered room and board for travelers. Political meetings were often held in public houses.

A favorite pipe
At public houses, the end piece of clay pipes were broken off so the next guest would have a fresh stem to smoke.

Wooden staves

Fill hole

Iron hoops bind wooden staves

Green-lead glass bottle

Corkscrew

Hungry for news
Patrons of a New York City coffeehouse read the newspapers, which might consist of recent editions published in the British-occupied city, month-old papers from England, or journals from rebel-held New Jersey.

A strong drink
Since water was often too polluted, brewed and distilled drinks quenched the thirst. Rum—stored in wooden kegs sealed by a cork—was very popular.

Hearth and home

Home life centered on the hearth, where food was cooked and hands were warmed. The hearth might be made of brick, cut stone, or dried clay, but it always had to have a ready supply of kindling and firewood—the task of the children, who fetched it from the woodshed.

Fitted bodice

Brown tabby silk material

A prized pitcher
Family heirlooms brought from Europe were treasured and handed down through the generations. This Rhenish pitcher was probably brought over from Germany.

Practical but graceful
The woman's everyday dress of the period had a close-fitting bodice above a petticoat and full overskirt. This allowed freedom of movement while modestly concealing the woman's ankles.

Finely dressed colonial doll

The family meal
The women of the house were in charge of the kitchen and the hearth, and spent many hours preparing food, preserving fruits and vegetables, drying herbs, and smoking meat.

Camps and prisons

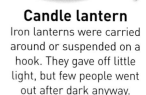

Door for replacing or extinguishing candle

Always short of money, both Congress and Parliament tried to avoid war expenses. This meant ignoring the needs of prisoners, who were often treated inhumanely. British prison ships were notoriously cruel, as were Patriot prison camps. It was no wonder that prisoners were badly cared for, since the enlisted soldier also was often neglected. While British soldiers were far better fed and equipped than Americans, both depended on their camp followers to give them comfort. The women and merchants following the armies provided food, drink, and welcome companionship to the off-duty soldier.

Candle lantern
Iron lanterns were carried around or suspended on a hook. They gave off little light, but few people went out after dark anyway.

Locked in a tower
A former Congress president, Henry Laurens was captured in 1780. He was thrown into the Tower of London and threatened with execution. Exchanged for General Cornwallis, Laurens went to Paris as a peace delegate.

Worthless money
Congress created its own money to be spent for the war effort. But many people did not want "Continental" money because if the rebels lost the war the money would become worthless.

Unloading supplies
Military encampments required a steady flow of loaded wagons to feed, clothe, shelter, and equip the troops. Sturdy Conestoga wagons pulled by teams of four to six oxen or horses were capable of hauling 15,000 lb (6,800 kg) of cargo over rough roads.

The fortunes of war

Prisons for the enlisted men of both sides were unhealthy, brutal places. Officers were treated far better, and were usually exchanged for an enemy prisoner of equal rank. The average soldier, however, was often left to rot for years, with a slim chance for survival or recovery.

Caverns called "Hell"
Just as horrific as British prison ships, the American prison in the copper mines of Newgate, Connecticut, took the lives or health of hundreds of captured Loyalists. Prisoners were forced to work deep beneath the surface in caverns they called "Hell."

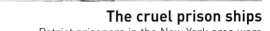

The cruel prison ships
Patriot prisoners in the New York area were crammed into old ships anchored around the city. These "prison hulks," such as the *Jersey*, anchored off Brooklyn, were damp, filthy, and cold, causing hundreds of starved prisoners to become ill and die.

Following the troops

Many civilians stayed close to the armies. These "camp followers" included wives and children of soldiers and merchants who sold wares to the troops. When not marching or fighting, soldiers had considerable freedom to visit their families among the camp followers, enjoying meals that were better than army fare.

Spoon carved from deer antler

Eating utensils
With long hours in camp, soldiers had time to carve bone and horn and whittle wood. They made utensils and cups, which were needed to replace utensils lost while campaigning.

Brass fork with wooden handle

Carved initials, "WCW"

Drinking cup made from a horn

Gridiron for cooking over campfire

Legs to stand over flame

Cooking for the troops
Camp followers were also found near prisoner-of-war enclosures, and a certain amount of communication was allowed between captives and their families. These folk cooked on open fires in their own encampments, often selling food to captive and sentry alike.

The soldier's doctor

In 1775, the colonies had about 3,500 doctors. The leading Patriot physician, Dr. Benjamin Rush of Philadelphia, wrote a manual on keeping soldiers healthy, but diseases like smallpox, typhus, and malaria killed 10 times more men than injuries sustained in battle. Hospitals were short-staffed and lacked supplies, medicine, and nutritious food. Conditions were primitive: surgical tools for extracting bullets, amputating limbs, and drawing blood were not sterilized. Many men died from minor, infected wounds. In time, better hospitals were designed, improving chances for recovery.

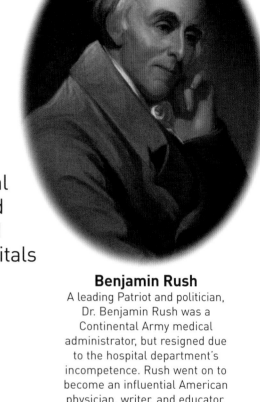

Benjamin Rush
A leading Patriot and politician, Dr. Benjamin Rush was a Continental Army medical administrator, but resigned due to the hospital department's incompetence. Rush went on to become an influential American physician, writer, and educator.

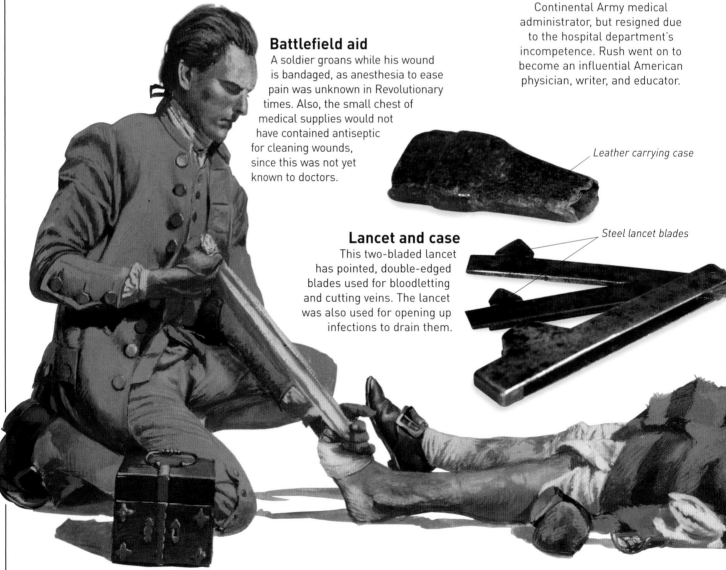

Battlefield aid
A soldier groans while his wound is bandaged, as anesthesia to ease pain was unknown in Revolutionary times. Also, the small chest of medical supplies would not have contained antiseptic for cleaning wounds, since this was not yet known to doctors.

Leather carrying case

Steel lancet blades

Lancet and case
This two-bladed lancet has pointed, double-edged blades used for bloodletting and cutting veins. The lancet was also used for opening up infections to drain them.

Improved hospitals

Replacing crowded sick chambers in tents and private homes, this Valley Forge hospital allowed the free flow of air, which helped improve patients' health.

The apothecary's art

Apothecaries made, mixed, and sold drugs, but most families used homegrown medicinal herbs. For serious illnesses, such as malaria, the apothecary used imported drugs.

Side compartments swing open on hinges, showing more storage space

Compartments for storing medicines

Portable medicine chest

Military physicians kept wooden chests containing medicines, syringes, sponges, forceps, bandages, twine, and pharmaceutical equipment for weighing and mixing ingredients. Hospitals used large chests, with 80 or more different medicines, while regimental surgeons in the field carried smaller chests.

Cupping glass

Medicine bottle

Medical equipment

Old bandages were pulled apart by iron forceps to see if the wound was healing. Placing a glass cup against the skin—"cupping"—drew blood and pus to the surface. A pewter bowl caught blood and fluids.

Pewter bowl

Cupping glass

Forceps

War for the South

Late in 1778, the war shifted to the South, as the British captured Savannah, Georgia. In the spring of 1780, Charleston, South Carolina, also fell to royal forces. General Cornwallis and his army soon destroyed an American force at Camden, South Carolina. George Washington sent Nathanael Greene of Rhode Island to take charge in the South. He lost several battles, but other American commanders won important victories. In March 1781, Cornwallis defeated Greene at Guilford Court House, North Carolina, but suffered great losses. Cornwallis withdrew to the sea, and eventually to Yorktown, Virginia, to await support that never came.

Death of Pulaski
Polish volunteer, General Casimir Pulaski, was killed leading a charge at the 1779 Siege of Savannah, a defeat for an army of Americans and French. He had fought with the American army since 1777, including at battles in Germantown and Brandywine.

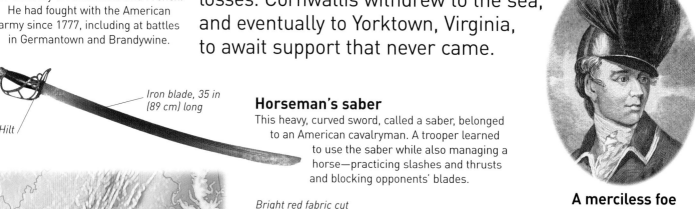

Iron blade, 35 in (89 cm) long

Hilt

Horseman's saber
This heavy, curved sword, called a saber, belonged to an American cavalryman. A trooper learned to use the saber while also managing a horse—practicing slashes and thrusts and blocking opponents' blades.

Bright red fabric cut from the back of a chair

Dragoon flag
This flag was carried into the Battle of Cowpens by Colonel William Washington's dragoons, who followed it to a smashing victory.

A merciless foe
Named "Butcher" by the Americans for his ruthless policy of taking no prisoners, British dragoon commander Lieutenant Colonel Banastre Tarleton served throughout the war.

The Roman numeral "VII" shows this is the flag of the 7th Fusiliers

Battles in the South
The British won most battles in the South, including Savannah, Charleston, and Camden. Still, Commander Greene organized fresh resistance wherever the enemy marched.

Captured colors
At Cowpens, General Morgan's troops captured the regimental flag of the British 7th Fusiliers, the proud Redcoat professionals. On the British side, more than 320 soldiers either died or were wounded, while 600 others were taken prisoner. In contrast, American casualties were 22 killed and 60 wounded.

Regimental badge

Cavalry fight at Cowpens, South Carolina

British dragoons surrounded American commander Colonel William Washington, center. His servant, left, fired a pistol and saved his life. Tarleton's 1,100-man British and Loyalist army was wiped out by an American force of about the same size under General Daniel Morgan.

Servant rescuing William Washington

The key to final victory

One of Washington's best generals in the South, Nathanael Greene kept his men fighting and avoided crushing defeats. While the British army pursued him, other rebel commanders attacked enemy supply lines and forts. By late 1781, almost all British posts outside Charleston and Savannah had been abandoned.

Victory in defeat

In 1781, Greene's force of 4,400 Continentals and militia took on Cornwallis's 1,900 men at Guilford Court House, North Carolina. After the furious battle, Cornwallis held the field but suffered more than 500 casualties. Greene lost fewer men—78 were killed and 183 wounded.

Winning the South

Nathanael Greene commanded rebel forces in the South. He inflicted very heavy losses on Cornwallis, who withdrew to Yorktown in 1781, hoping for reinforcements.

Lid *Forest motifs*

Cartridge box

This brass cartridge box was probably once the property of a German soldier. It kept ammunition safe and dry.

Shot bags

Revolutionary militia soldiers sometimes took hunting firearms into battle. These leather shot bags held five bird-shot balls.

Plug top

Yorktown

By August 1781, Cornwallis and his 7,500 veterans were at Yorktown, Virginia, waiting for reinforcements and supplies from British-held New York. Washington and French general De Rochambeau moved to trap Cornwallis, and the French fleet arrived to blockade Yorktown. The Franco-American armies numbered more than 17,000 troops. The British fleet arrived in September, but the French admiral De Grasse drove it back to New York. Washington fired devastating artillery barrages day after day, until Cornwallis gave up. On October 19, the defeated royal army marched out of Yorktown. This was the last major battle of the Revolution.

Washington at Yorktown
Riding alongside Marquis de Lafayette, his dependable young general, George Washington directs American and French troops in this folk art painting of the Yorktown victory.

Pocket telescope
Telescopes were essential for military leaders to view enemy troop movements. They were also used on ships to observe flag signals from friendly vessels.

Eyepiece

Lens

Screw cap protects lens

Sir Samuel Hood
British Admiral Hood, alongside Admiral Thomas Graves, could not prevent the French navy from blockading Cornwallis, who was trapped.

Francois de Grasse
French warships under Admiral de Grasse landed 3,000 soldiers to help besiege the British at Yorktown in September 1781. When enemy ships appeared, de Grasse fought them off.

The decisive sea battle
Admiral de Grasse beat British admirals Hood and Graves at the Battle of the Chesapeake Capes on September 15, forcing them back to New York. If the British Navy had brought reinforcements or rescued Cornwallis, this campaign could have turned in favor of the British.

Storming the Yorktown redoubt

Washington moved his trenches and artillery closer to the British fortifications by digging new works under cover of darkness. On October 14, Captain Alexander Hamilton led a nighttime assault against a British redoubt, while French infantry attacked another. Eventually, Cornwallis had to surrender.

Artilleryman's linstock

Gunners at Yorktown used a linstock like this to hold the match that fired a cannon. The match was brought to the touch hole, igniting the gunpowder that fired the charge.

Spear point

Iron linstock piece is 14 in (36 cm) long

Match rope

Wooden shaft

Charles Cornwallis

Lord Cornwallis won battles but could not destroy the rebels. After the war, he became governor general of India and a high official in the British government.

The deadly bayonet

At the start of the Revolution, a bayonet wielded by a Redcoat was the most feared of weapons. By the war's end, elite American troops were also skilled in bayonet attacks. This was how they captured a key stronghold at Yorktown.

Washington's greatest victory

Claiming illness, Cornwallis did not attend the surrender ceremonies, so his second-in-command offered his sword to Washington. He refused it, and directed the sword to his own second-in-command.

The last two years of war

Although the battles ended with Yorktown, the war would not be over until the peace was signed. There were small clashes, and men still died. Washington promised to remain in the field until New York City, the last Redcoat foothold, was evacuated. Through much of 1782–1783, he was with his army near Newburgh, New York. Still, his officers and men were angry that Congress was unable to provide the back pay it owed them. So, in part to lift their spirits, Washington created a decoration, later known as the "Purple Heart."

Loss of life continues
A much-admired aide to Washington, Colonel John Laurens was killed during a minor clash near Charleston in his native South Carolina. Laurens was the son of Henry Laurens, former president of Congress.

The official seal
Congress agreed in 1782 on a concept for America's seal, based on Secretary of Congress Charles Thomson's above sketch. The motto "E Pluribus Unum" means "One out of many."

Various caliber lead bullets

Hudson headquarters
Washington could have gone home to Mount Vernon during the winter of 1782–1783, but he stayed with the army instead. The Americans were based close to Newburgh, New York, about 50 miles (80 km) north of British-held New York City. The general lived in the Hasbrouck house, next to the Hudson River.

A casualty's hat
Connecticut militiaman Phineas Meigs was 74 when he answered an alarm in 1782. As a British warship was raiding East Guilford, he was shot in the head. He was one of the last to die in the Revolution.

The soldiers go home

The Continental Army was disbanded in stages during 1783. Although officially discharged, they did not get the back pay owed to them because Congress lacked the funds. The troops were discharged a few at a time to avoid an angry mass mutiny by the unhappy men. Many returned home embittered that Congress had not kept its promises. Years would pass before the soldiers received their long-deserved pay and pensions.

A Loyalist's coat

Munson Hoyt of Norwalk, Connecticut, owner of this coat, was a Loyalist lieutenant. He relocated to New Brunswick, Canada, but eventually returned to live in the United States.

Farewells at New Windsor

Revolutionary troops above leave their quarters at New Windsor, New York. The Hudson Highlands in the background provided them with a strong position to prevent the British from striking northward from New York City.

Sir Guy Carleton

Carleton replaced Clinton as the commander of British forces in America. Carleton worked closely with Washington to arrange a peaceful evacuation of Redcoats from New York in November 1783.

Liberty handkerchief

This printed linen handkerchief has 13 hearts for the new states and bears illustrations of domestic scenes. Its 13 verses honor soldiers at war and families working at home: "While they our Liberties defend/Let us to Husbandry attend."

Thirteen hearts

Stanzas of verse

Domestic scenes

The purple heart

Washington created a "Badge of Military Merit" to award soldiers for outstanding acts of courage. Only three such badges were awarded, all in 1783. It was almost forgotten until 1932, the 200th anniversary of Washington's birth, when it was reactivated as the "Purple Heart," a decoration for individuals wounded in action.

Design of original purple heart

Modern-day purple heart

Badge of Military Merit

Washington awards the new badges at his Newburgh, New York, headquarters in 1783. Sergeant William Brown receives his badge, while Sergeant Elijah Churchill awaits. Sergeant Daniel Bissell was honored later.

The birth of a nation

From mid-1782 until September 1783, British and American delegates in Paris negotiated peace terms. The final 1783 Treaty of Paris recognized the independence of the United States, with the Mississippi River as its western boundary. It took several years, however, before a Constitution was drafted that all the states could accept.

One of the most important leaders in this period was the political thinker James Madison, who helped write the Constitution. The Constitution of the United States was drafted in 1787 and went into effect on March 4, 1789 as the central law of the new nation.

Locket of remembrance
During the Revolution, Patriot John Adams of Massachusetts was often away from his beloved wife, Abigail. When he went to Paris to negotiate peace, he gave this locket to her.

Provisional agreement
In November 1782, a provisional peace treaty to end the Revolutionary War was signed by the negotiators. The final document was approved on September 3, 1783, and named the Treaty of Paris.

American peacemakers
Artist Benjamin West painted portraits of the American peace negotiators in Paris to include them in a larger painting along with British negotiators. However, the British refused to pose, so West left them out of this picture. The Americans are, from left to right, John Jay, John Adams, Benjamin Franklin, Henry Laurens, and William Temple Franklin, their secretary.

Washington submits his resignation

At the height of his glory as a conquering hero, George Washington faithfully returned his commander in chief's commission to members of Congress assembled at Annapolis, Maryland, on December 23, 1783.

The Constitution

On September 17, 1787— four years after the end of the Revolutionary War—representatives of the 13 states met in Philadelphia to approve an official Constitution. Establishing a federal system of government for the states, this document was declared "the supreme law of the land."

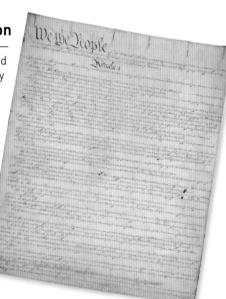

Symbol for the Society of the Cincinnati

General Lincoln's teapot

This teapot includes the symbol of the Society of the Cincinnati, a fraternity of Revolutionary officers. It bears the initials "BL," honoring General Benjamin Lincoln.

James Madison

The cornerstone of the new American republic was its Constitution, and Virginian James Madison was a key author of this document. In time, he would become the fourth president of the United States.

Revolutionary financier

Philadelphia merchant Robert Morris was an early Patriot leader who headed the Continental Congress's Department of Finance during the war. He also helped lay the foundation for the financial operations of the new United States.

Territorial claims

Many states claimed to own western lands, but these claims were eventually turned over to the federal government. This map shows those claims in a tint of the same color as that of the claiming state.

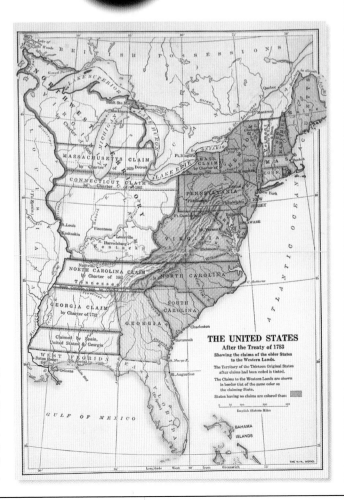

THE UNITED STATES
After the Treaty of 1783

Showing the claims of the older States to the Western Lands.

The Territory of the Thirteen Original States after claims had been ceded is tinted.

The Claims to the Western Lands are shown in border tint of the same color as the claiming State.

States having no claims are colored thus:

George Washington

Early in December 1783, Washington bade farewell to his officers. Among them was General Henry Knox, one of the first to call Washington the "Father of His Country." A few weeks later, Washington resigned his commission before Congress and rode back to his wife, Martha, in Mount Vernon. But he was called back, becoming the first president of the United States from 1789–1797. The first capital was in New York City and was then changed to Philadelphia. After his presidency, Washington enjoyed the life of a Virginia planter. On December 14, 1799, he died at Mount Vernon.

Washington in victory
Patriot artist Charles Willson Peale created this image of the general a few months after the 1779 liberation of Philadelphia. The painting commemorates Washington's victory at Princeton two years earlier.

The general's pistols
Washington owned this pair of silver-mounted pistols during the Revolution. Made in England, they bear designs that include the lion and the unicorn.

Silver decoration with the lion and the unicorn

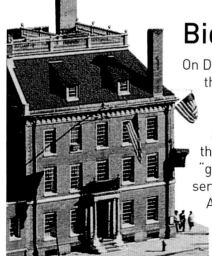

Bidding farewell

On December 4, 1783—after the British evacuated New York City—Washington and his officers gathered at Fraunces Tavern. He thanked them for their "glorious and honorable" service. Then, he rode to Annapolis, Maryland, and resigned as commander in chief. On this journey, people lined the roads to see him.

The Fraunces Tavern Museum

Washington's farewell to his officers in Fraunces Tavern

Signing the Constitution

Washington was elected presiding officer of the Constitutional Convention in Philadelphia. On September 28, 1787, as pictured above, the delegates signed the document. In 1789, Washington became the first president of the United States.

Stately Mount Vernon

Washington inherited Mount Vernon from his brother, Lawrence, who built it. When Washington married Martha Custis, who owned several estates, he brought her to Mount Vernon to live.

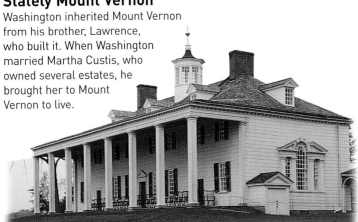

Home at Mount Vernon

Whether in military headquarters or serving as the United States president, Washington often longed to be with Martha in Mount Vernon. He loved his estate that overlooked the Potomac River. He managed Mount Vernon's agriculture, selected the crops, and planned development. The Washingtons were the guardians of two of their grandchildren, who enriched their home life.

George Washington's grandchildren

The Virginia planter

Washington enjoyed working on his plantation. Mount Vernon's fields were tended by slaves, who—in accord with Washington's will—were given their freedom after he and Martha died.

Reflector

Martha Custis Washington

Martha Washington was known for her kindness and wisdom. She carried herself with the natural style and grace that befitted the first First Lady of the United States.

Washington's candelabrum

Porcelain serving dish from Mount Vernon

Did you know?

FASCINATING FACTS

In 1778, John Adams took his young son, John Quincy Adams, with him to England. In 1781, at age 14, the younger Adams was appointed secretary and translator to the US commissioner to the Court of Russia.

Young John Quincy Adams

During the Revolution, soldiers tore paper out of books to use as wadding to clean out their rifles.

Rebels imprisoned Benjamin Franklin's son William, Royal Governor of New Jersey. He remained a Loyalist and fled to England in 1782.

In 1775, Benjamin Franklin wrote a Declaration of Independence. It would be another year before Congress would ask Thomas Jefferson to write his version—with Franklin's help.

Although it is not certain that Betsy Ross sewed the first American flag, she did mend uniforms and make tents, blankets, musket balls, and gun cartridges.

On April 26, 1777, Sybil Ludington, age 16, rode 20 miles (32 km) to alert her father's militia company that Danbury, Connecticut, was under attack and to gather at the Ludington house. George Washington later thanked her.

Many women came under fire in war, like Margaret Corbin, who was wounded serving in the Battle of Fort Washington on November 16, 1776.

Most people know about the Boston Tea Party of 1773. But few people remember that on March 7, 1774, protesters dumped more tea in the harbor at a second "party."

In 1776, Americans had the highest standard of living and the lowest taxes in the Western world.

Washington was hesitant at first about enlisting blacks, but the impressive fighting of black troops at Bunker Hill helped change his mind. By 1779, about one in seven Americans in Washington's army was black.

Two brothers from Virginia, Richard Henry Lee and Francis Lightfoot Lee, were among the signers of the Declaration of Independence. Their cousin, Revolutionary War commander Henry Lee, was the father of Robert E. Lee, who would command the Confederate Army during the American Civil War.

The American uniforms during the war were blue because indigo was one of the most common dyes available in the colonies.

Indigo blue

American uniform

Before the Battle of Trenton, a boy handed Colonel Johann Gottlieb Rall a note warning that Washington was about to attack. He put the note in his pocket unopened; it was found after he was killed in the battle.

The Battle of Rhode Island

QUESTIONS AND ANSWERS

Q What is the Society of the Cincinatti?

A General Henry Knox founded this society after the Revolutionary War. It was made up of the officers who served in the Continental Army.

Q Why did King George III of England nearly abdicate the throne?

A Parliament did not adhere to the king's wish to fight after Yorktown. So, the king wrote a letter of abdication, but later withdrew it. He hoped that Washington would become a dictator, making Americans resent their new leader. When he learned that Washington would resign, the king exclaimed, "If he does that, Sir, he will be the greatest man in the world!"

Q Where did the song "Yankee Doodle" come from?

A Richard Shuckburgh, an English surgeon in New York, is thought to have written some of the most famous verses. His "Yankey Song" made fun of New England militiamen in the French and Indian War. The term "Yankee" comes from the Dutch word "Janke," or "Johnny." "Doodle" meant fool, or clown. By 1776, the Patriots had their own version.

Q When was the first official name given to the United States?

A On September 9, 1776, the Continental Congress officially declared the name of the new nation the United States of North America. Two years later, Congress officially decided to shorten the name to the United States of America.

Q When did the eagle become an American symbol?

A The bald eagle became an official symbol in 1782. Congress put it on the Great Seal of the United States.

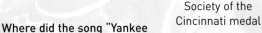

Bald eagle

Society of the
Cincinnati medal

Q Why is there a monument to an unnamed soldier's left leg on the battlefield at Saratoga?

A Although he later helped the British, Benedict Arnold was a great American hero at Saratoga. During the battle, a bullet shattered his left leg. A monument was built at Saratoga to honor him, but planners decided not to show his name, since he was by then considered a traitor.

Q Which one of Washington's children died at the Battle of Yorktown?

A Washington did not have his own natural children, but he adopted Martha's children after their marriage. His adopted son, John "Jackie" Parke Custis, was an aide to Washington at the Battle of Yorktown. Sadly, he died of camp fever after the battle ended.

John Parke Custis

Q Did George Washington really have wooden teeth?

A No. According to legend, he never smiled in paintings because he was embarrassed about his wooden teeth. He did have such bad toothaches that his real teeth were pulled and replaced with false ones, but they were not made of wood. During his life he had several pairs of dentures. The last ones that he owned were carved from hippopotamus ivory with a palate made from a sheet of gold and springs made of coiled gold wire.

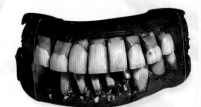

George Washington's
false teeth

Q What did George Washington state about the slaves on his plantation in his will?

A He stated that all of his slaves and their children were to be freed upon his death. Those belonging to Martha's first husband were freed later.

Washington with two of his slaves

Timeline

Grand Union flag

On July 4, 1776, when representatives of the 13 British colonies signed the Declaration of Independence, it was far from certain that they could win that independence. But the Americans knew how to fight. When they defeated the British at the Battle of Saratoga in 1777, the tide began to turn. Still, it would be six more years before a peace was reached and the new nation found its freedom.

A Hessian cap

NOVEMBER 1, 1765 Riots break out in New York and Boston in protest over the Stamp Act, which requires colonists to pay taxes on printed matter, legal documents, and even playing cards.

MARCH 5, 1770 The Boston Massacre takes place when a group of Patriots throws chunks of ice, oyster shells, and other items at British soldiers. The soldiers fire into the crowd, killing five.

DECEMBER 16, 1773 The Boston Tea Party occurs when Patriots dress as Indians, storm British ships, and throw their cargo of tea into Boston Harbor.

SEPTEMBER 5, 1774 After the port of Boston closes, delegates from all colonies, except Georgia, hold the First Continental Congress in Philadelphia to petition King George III of England formally to hear their grievances.

APRIL 18–19, 1775 Paul Revere tells John Hancock and Samuel Adams that British troops are planning to ambush the Patriots. He is captured after reaching Concord and later released.

Montgomery's death at the Battle of Quebec

APRIL 19, 1775 Colonial militiamen halt advancing British troops at Lexington Common, Massachusetts, as the Revolutionary War begins.

JUNE 17, 1775 Although the British take heavy losses during the battles of Bunker Hill and Breed's Hill near Boston, they still take control of the city.

NOVEMBER–DECEMBER 1775 Patriots capture Montreal from British forces, but are defeated at Quebec City on December 31. During the battle, Patriot commander Richard Montgomery is killed by cannon fire.

JANUARY 1, 1776 To celebrate the formation of the Continental Army, Washington flies the Grand Union flag near his Massachusetts headquarters.

JULY 4, 1776 Thomas Jefferson's draft of the Declaration of Independence is approved by the Second Continental Congress. Some delegates fear that it will unite Britain against them and lead to their destruction.

Redcoats at Bunker Hill

AUGUST 29–30, 1776 British and Hessian forces beat Washington's soldiers at Brooklyn, New York. Washington retreats to New York City and directs officer Nathan Hale to disguise himself as a schoolmaster and look for intelligence about the British. Hale is caught and hanged.

JUNE 14, 1777 Congress declares that "the flag of the United States be made of thirteen stripes, alternate red and white; that the union be thirteen stars, white in a blue field, representing a new Constellation."

OCTOBER 4, 1777 At the Battle of Germantown, in Pennsylvania, Washington attacks British troops under Sir William Howe. The attack fails and he is forced to retreat. Howe is forced to resign after he spends the winter in Philadelphia instead of pursuing Patriots.

OCTOBER 17, 1777 General Burgoyne's British troops are defeated near Saratoga, New York.

DECEMBER 1777–MARCH 1778 The Continental Army spends a harsh winter at Valley Forge, Pennsylvania.

Henry Clinton

MARCH 7, 1778 Henry Clinton replaces William Howe as the commander of British troops in America.

DECEMBER 29, 1778 The British capture and occupy Savannah, Georgia.

FEBRUARY 25, 1779 On the Wabash River, General George Rogers Clark's troops capture Fort Vincennes from the British.

SEPTEMBER 23, 1780 Two days after General Benedict Arnold gives military secrets to British Major John André, André is captured, and Arnold flees to the British side.

OCTOBER 7, 1780 Americans defeat Scottish-led Loyalists at King's Mountain, North Carolina.

JANUARY 17, 1781 Americans beat the British at Cowpens, South Carolina.

JANUARY 1781 Washington puts down rebellions by New Jersey and Pennsylvania regiments over lack of pay and low rations. However, they continue to fight the British.

MARCH 2, 1781 The Articles of Confederation go into effect in all 13 colonies.

MARCH 15, 1781 British general Lord Cornwallis defeats the colonials at Guilford Court House, North Carolina, then retreats to Yorktown, Virginia.

A tin canteen used at the Battle of Germantown

Powder horn carried at King's Mountain

OCTOBER 19, 1781 At the Siege of Yorktown in Virginia, British commander Lord Cornwallis surrenders to George Washington. Cornwallis sends his second in command to accept surrender.

APRIL 1, 1782 Washington settles his army near Newburgh, New York, to await the surrender of New York City.

NOVEMBER 30, 1782 In Paris, British delegates negotiate peace terms with an American team led by Benjamin Franklin and John Adams.

SEPTEMBER 3, 1783 Britain and the United States sign the Treaty of Paris, agreeing that all British troops will leave US territory and that US lands will extend to the Mississippi River in the West, the Great Lakes and St. Lawrence River in the North, excluding the Spanish territories of Florida and West Florida in the South.

NOVEMBER 25, 1783 The last British soldiers leave New York.

DECEMBER 23, 1783 Washington returns his commander in chief's commission to Congress, at Annapolis, Maryland, and returns to his home.

France's navy blockades Yorktown

Find out more

The American Revolution was fought throughout the original colonies, as well as in Ohio, Indiana, Florida, and even Canada. Visitors today can see the forts and battlefields where soldiers fought, and the weapons, uniforms, and personal possessions used during the war.

Cannon

Washington's writing desk

Big guns of Fort Ticonderoga
During the 1775–1776 winter, Fort Ticonderoga's arsenal included more than 60 heavy cannon and mortars. Today, "Fort Ti" welcomes over 90,000 visitors each year, who can see one of the world's largest collections of 18th-century artillery.

Washington slept here
Visitors to the Colonial National Historical Park in Yorktown, Virginia, can see tents like this one used by George Washington at the Siege of Yorktown in 1781. After touring the site of the Revolution's last major battle, be sure to visit nearby Colonial Williamsburg, the world's largest living history museum.

USEFUL WEBSITES

- The National Museum of American History has many items from Revolution-era America: **americanhistory.si.edu**
- The National Park Service's fact-filled site on the Revolution lets you tour places and view objects: **www.nps.gov/revwar**
- A companion website to the PBS series on the American Revolution: **www.pbs.org/ktca/liberty**
- A very thorough site with hundreds of helpful links: **www.americanrevolution.com**
- Learn about the Declaration of Independence at the National Archives: **www.archives.gov**

Birthplace of independence
Visitors to Philadelphia can explore Independence Hall, where the Declaration of Independence and the Constitution were signed.

Artist Robert Wilson

Robert Wilson's son

History in art

This painting by Robert Wilson is on display at the Ninety Six Historical Site in South Carolina. Robert Wilson spent more than 500 hours researching and working on the painting. Before finishing it, he painted himself and his son into the action.

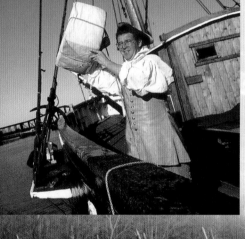

Tea time

Each year on December 16, performers dress as Indians to reenact the Boston Tea Party of 1773. Visitors to the Boston Tea Party Ship and Museum in Boston Harbor can tour a life-sized replica of one of the ships and even hurl a bale of "tea" over the side of the boat!

PLACES TO VISIT

MORRISTOWN NATIONAL HISTORICAL PARK MORRISTOWN, NEW JERSEY

This area was used twice as the Continental Army's winter encampment. It includes Washington's headquarters.

COLONIAL WILLIAMSBURG WILLIAMSBURG, VIRGINIA

Colonial Williamsburg is the world's largest living history museum.

MOORES CREEK NATIONAL BATTLEFIELD CURRIE, NORTH CAROLINA

Visit the site where the march of North Carolina Loyalists was stopped by Patriot cannon fire in February 1776.

ADAMS NATIONAL HISTORICAL PARK QUINCY, MASSACHUSETTS

Don't miss the reenactment of the Declaration of Independence's historic passage at the home of five generations of Adamses, which included two presidents.

ARKANSAS POST NATIONAL MEMORIAL GILLETT, ARKANSAS

The "Colbert Raid" in 1783 was the only Revolutionary War battle in Arkansas.

INDIAN MILL STATE MEMORIAL UPPER SANDUSKY, OHIO

In June 1782, 500 Patriots battled British and Indians here. A museum in an old gristmill is a highlight.

FORT BOONESBOROUGH STATE PARK RICHMOND, KENTUCKY

In 1778, this fort bore a nine-day attack by Indians and Frenchmen.

Patriots' Day

A Massachusetts state holiday commemorates the Battles of Lexington and Concord each year on April 19, when the first shots of the war were fired. A great place for your Patriots' Day celebration is Minuteman National Historic Park in Lexington and Concord, where families can watch actors in full costume honor that historic day.

Glossary

APOTHECARY A person, such as a pharmacist, who prepares and sells medicines and drugs.

APPRENTICE A person who learns a trade from another person.

ARTILLERY Mounted guns or the group of soldiers or branch of the military that use these weapons.

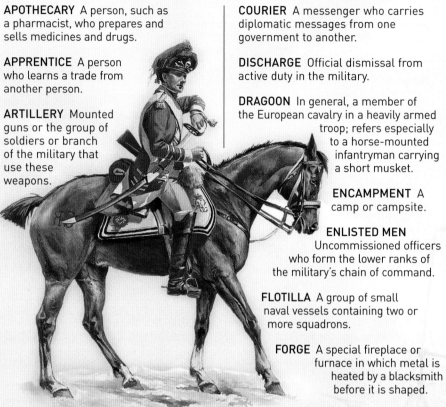

Dragoon

BARRACKS A building, or buildings, in a military garrison used to house soldiers.

BLACK POWDER An explosive powder made up of saltpeter, sulfur, and charcoal.

BLOCKADE The blocking of traffic, usually by sea, going into or out of a place, such as a seaport. Blockades were set up during war to prevent weapons and supplies from entering an enemy location.

BOYCOTT An organized effort to stop using a certain kind of item, like English tea, to win a change in policy.

BOMBARD To attack with artillery fire.

BUCKSKIN The skin of a buck, or male deer, often used for clothing.

CALIBER The diameter of a gun's interior barrel.

CANDELABRUM A candleholder.

CORONATION The act of crowning a king, queen, or other ruler.

COURIER A messenger who carries diplomatic messages from one government to another.

DISCHARGE Official dismissal from active duty in the military.

DRAGOON In general, a member of the European cavalry in a heavily armed troop; refers especially to a horse-mounted infantryman carrying a short musket.

ENCAMPMENT A camp or campsite.

ENLISTED MEN Uncommissioned officers who form the lower ranks of the military's chain of command.

FLOTILLA A group of small naval vessels containing two or more squadrons.

FORGE A special fireplace or furnace in which metal is heated by a blacksmith before it is shaped.

FORTIFICATION The act of fortifying or strengthening.

FUSILIER A soldier in the British army armed with fusils, a type of light flintlock musket.

GARRISON A permanent military post.

HOWITZER A small cannon or large caliber gun with a short barrel.

INDIGO A plant with red or purple flowers that are used to make blue dye; it is native in the Southern colonies.

LOOTING To carry off or steal.

LOUIS D'OR A French coin named after King Louis XIII; France stopped making them in 1795, after the French Revolution.

Pistol

LOYALIST (or **TORY**) A colonist who remained loyal to Great Britain and opposed the drive for independence. About one-fifth of all citizens of the colonies were Loyalists.

MALARIA A deadly disease spread by mosquitoes.

MILITIA A group of ordinary citizens not part of the regular army that is called into emergency military service.

MORTAR A type of cannon with a very short barrel but very wide bore, used for launching mortar shells at high angles.

MUSKET A smoothbore, single-shot, muzzle-loading shoulder gun. Infantrymen could fire three shots per minute from a flintlock musket. A long, triangular-shaped bayonet could be attached to the barrel to use as a weapon when the enemy was at arm's length.

MUSTER To assemble for battle, inspection, or roll call.

MUTINY An organized rebellion by a group of soldiers against the commanding officer or officers.

NATURAL RIGHTS A term referring to rights that a person is born with, or that are granted by God.

NEUTRAL Not taking sides, especially between two sides in a military conflict.

PARLIAMENT The national legislature of Great Britain, made up of the House of Commons and the House of Lords.

PATRIOT Those colonists during the Revolution who were active in fighting for independence.

PENCE The plural form of a British penny. Twelve pence equalled a shilling, and there were 20 shillings in a pound.

PETITION A written statement or plea, signed by a group of people that oppose a particular policy, requesting or demanding a change in that policy.

PILLAGE To strip of money or possessions by using violence, especially during war.

PISTOL A short gun that is designed to be aimed and fired with one hand.

Philipsburg Manor, a plantation in upstate New York

PLANTATION A farm where cotton, tobacco, coffee, rice, hops, and other crops are grown as cash crops and where the workforce lives on site.

PROPAGANDA Information or ideas that are spread to others with the purpose of either promoting or hampering a cause.

PUBLIC HOUSE A tavern or inn, often used for political meetings during the Revolution.

REALES Silver Spanish coins that were worth one eighth of a peso.

REINFORCEMENTS Additional troops or ships.

REGIMENT A military unit made up of two or more smaller battle groups called battalions, as well as a headquarters group and other supporting groups.

SABER A heavy sword with one sharp edge, usually curved, that was used by cavalrymen.

"SC 3" markings for South Carolina, 3rd Regiment

A jacket button for a South Carolina regiment

Saber

SHARPSHOOTER A person who shoots a gun with especially good aim.

SIEGE A military maneuver in which one force surrounds or blockades a fortification so that supplies will be cut from the outside, hopefully leading to a surrender.

SMALLPOX A deadly and highly contagious disease that causes fever and skin blisters.

SMOOTHBORE Refers to a gun with a smooth bore (inside barrel surface).

SOAPSTONE A soft mineral that has a soapy feel, used as material for bullet molds, fireplaces, and sinks.

SQUADRONS A group of two or more divisions of a fleet of ships.

SURVEYOR A person who takes exact measurements in order to determine the boundaries, area, and elevation of a certain piece of land.

THEATER OF ACTION A general zone of sustained military action.

THEORIST A person who deals with concepts or explanations behind an idea.

TOMAHAWK A small ax used by Native American warriors as a weapon or tool.

Union Jack

TRICORN A popular Revolutionary-era hat, in which the brim is turned up on three sides to form corners.

TURNCOAT A traitor.

TYPHUS A deadly disease caused by organisms, such as fleas and ticks; common in the crowded and unclean encampments of the Revolutionary War.

UNION JACK A popular term for the national flag of Great Britain. It is made up of a red and white cross representing England, a diagonal white cross representing Scotland, and a diagonal red cross representing Ireland.

VOLUNTEER A person who offers his or her service freely.

Index

Acknowledgments

The author and publisher offer their grateful thanks to: Ellen Nanney and Robyn Bissette of the Product Development and Licensing Department of the Smithsonian Institution; Barbara Clark Smith, Jennifer L. Jones, Marko Zlatich, and Lisa Kathleen Graddy of the National Museum of American History, Behring Center; Catherine H. Grosfils, Colonial Williamsburg Foundation; Christopher D. Fox, Fort Ticonderoga Museum; Joan Bacharach and Khaled Bassim, National Park Service, Museum Management Program; Carol Haines, Concord Museum (www.concordmuseum.org); Peter Harrington, Anne S.K. Brown Military Collection; Richard Malley, Connecticut Historical Society; Andrea Ashby, Independence National Historical Park; Claudia Jew, The Mariners' Museum; and Tordis Isselhardt, Images from the Past; Ashwin Khurana for text editing.

Photography Credits:
t = top; b = bottom; l = left; r = right; c = center
Abby Aldrich Rockefeller Folk Art Museum, Williamsburg, VA: 7tr, 39bl. Adams National Historical Park: 60tl. *The American Revolution*, by John Fiske: 8tl, 12cl, 13bc, 18cr, 28cr, 31tr, 41br, 42cl, 44c, 46tr, 47bc, 47br, 54cr, 56bl, 56cr, 57bl,

58tr, 59cr. Anne S.K. Brown Military Collection, Brown University Library: 12bl, 17t, 18tl, 18-19t, 19bl, 27b. Boston National Historical Park: 19br. Boston Tea Party Chapter, DAR: 11cl. © David Cain: 8tr, 24bl. Center of Military History, H. Charles McBarron: 24tr, 31bl, 32b, 35br, 55cr, 57t, 59br. The Charleston Museum: 7c, 7cr. The Colonel Charles Waterhouse Historical Museum: 20b, 25b, 36bl, 41t. Colonial Williamsburg Foundation: 7bl, 7br, 10t, 12br, 12tr, 14c, 15c, 23cl, 44cl, 46cr, 48cl, 49bl, 49bc, 49br, 51br, 53tr, 56tr, 61cr. Concord Museum, Concord, Massachusetts: 16tc, 39tc, 59c, 61tr. Connecticut Historical Society: 16bl, 16cl, 19cl, 19tr, 24c, 46tl, 48b, 51tl, 58cl, 59tl. Dahl Taylor: 6tl. © David R. Wagner, 1994: 64b. Delaware Art Museum: 66b. Painting by Don Troiani, www.historicalartprints.com: 70tl. Photos courtesy of Don Troiani, www.historicalartprints.com: 66tl, 67tr, 67tl, 70b, 71cl, 71b. Dover Publications: 15tl, 21tr, 31tl, 34b, 42bc, 44bl, 44tl, 46bl. Fort Ticonderoga Museum: 9c, 9cr, 15tc, 17tl, 17br, 17cr, 19c, 22c, 22tr, 46c, 68tr. © The Frick Collection, New York: 32tl. Photo courtesy of Ian Britton: 68-69; Independence National Historical Park: 13c, 13cr, 13br, 21cr, 27c, 27bl, 31tl, 36tr, 39tr, 52tr, 55bl, 68b. The Institute

of Heraldry: 59bl, 59cl (drawing by James Burmester). James Burmester: 66; Library of Congress: 7cl, 8cl, 9br, 10b, 11b, 11tc, 11tr, 12bc, 14bl, 15bc, 15bl, 18b, 19tc, 22b, 23tl, 24br, 26br, 27br, 29b, 29cr, 29tl, 33cl, 34tr, 35bl, 36cr, 38cl, 39tl, 40br, 42bl, 42br, 42tr, 45b, 45cr, 45tr, 47t, 51tr, 53tl, 54tl, 55t, 58b, 59tr, 61bl, 61c, 62br, 63cr, 65bl, 67bl, 67br. Lexington, Massachusetts Historical Society: 17c, 17cl. Marblehead Historical Society, Marblehead, MA: 6c. The Mariners' Museum, Newport News, VA: 9t, 38tl, 43t, 43br, 56br. Massachusetts Historical Society: 10cr. Morristown National Historical Park: 44br. Mount Vernon Ladies' Association: 13tl, 65tr, 65br. MPI Archives: 7tl, 40bl, 63cl. National Archives: 16tl, 58tl, 60tr. National Museum of American History: 6bl, 6br, 9cl, 10cl, 15br, 21bl, 25c, 25t, 26c, 29tc, 34tl, 39br, 63bc, 63br, 64tr, 68tl. National Numismatics Collection: 40cb, 40ct, 43bc, 43bl, 50bl, 50cl. National Park Service: 21cl, 20tr, 31c, 37tr, 37b, 37c, 53ct. National Park Service, Don Troiani: 20tl, 22cr, 22tl, 23b, 23tc, 35tr, 37tl, 50br, 52-53bb, 54bc, 54br. National Park Service, Museum Management Program and Guilford Courthouse National Military Park, photos by Khaled Bassim: 28tr, 28cl, 41c, 45c, 45cl, 45tc, 45tl, 48tr, 49crb, 49crt, 49r, 49tr, 50tr, 51bc, 51bl, 52cb, 52ct, 53bl, 53br, 53cb, 55bc, 55br, 57cr, 58ct. National Park Service, Museum Management Program and Valley Forge National Historical Park, photos by Carol Highsmith and Khaled Bassim: 8cr, 9bl, 14br,

14cr, 15tr, 21br, 21tc, 21tl, 23c, 23cl, 23cr, 29tr, 30r, 31zr, 33tc, 33tl, 35cl, 35cr, 36bc, 36tl, 37cr, 41tr, 47bl, 51crb, 51crt, 54cl, 56cl, 57bc. National Portrait Gallery: 11tl, 13bl, 14tl, 26tr, 33tr, 35tl, 40tl, 41bl, 44cr, 46br, 50tl, 61br, 63bl, 64tl. Peter Newark's Pictures: 26bl. © Robert Holmes/CORBIS: 68–69c. Painting courtesy of Robert Wilson, Jr.: 69t; © Ron Toelke Associates: 30l, 32tr, 54bl. Smithsonian American Art Museum: 16br, 23tr. Society of the Cincinnati: 65tl. Sons of the Revolution in the State of New York, Inc./ Fraunces Tavern® Museum, New York City: 31br, 38-39b, 62bl. State Historical Society of Wisconsin: 8bl. U.S. Capitol: 27t, 33br, 57br, 61tl, 63t. U.S. Senate Collection: 28b, 62tr. ©1996, Virginia Historical Society, Lora Robins Collection of Virginia Art: 13tr. West Point Museum, Photos © Paul Warchol Photography, Inc.: 24cr, 33cr, 33bl, 62c. Winterthur Museum: 60b.

All other images © Dorling Kindersley.

For further information see:
www.dkimages.com